"As someone who has been active in trades' uni[...] tury, and who knows for herself how precaric[...] England, I was delighted that trades' unions were opening [...] Why is it so hard to evolve a committed and passionate institution that prioritizes equality and natural justice? The explorations in this book go some way to answering that question. Read. Be challenged. Be affirmed."

—**LINDA ISIORHO**, Anglican priest

"*Faith in Unions* is a forensic and prophetic exposé of the Church of England's betrayal of Christ, and its endemic culture of racism, abuse, and victimization of the whistleblowers of these offences. David Isiorho draws parallels between white Anglican-Methodist discrimination and bullying in the Unite Faith Workers' Union, and the identical collusion by the Church of England with secular bureaucrats and lawyers to harass and silence abuse victims and ethnic minority complainants."

—**MOHAMED ELSHARKAWY**, Al-Azhar College

"*Faith in Unions* reveals the deep and insidious reach of institutional racism in the UK. David Isiorho's compelling recounting of his experience of racism is a searing, incisive, and necessary reading. While calling both his ecclesial tradition and the Faith Workers' Branch of Unite to account, Isiorho's commitment as a priest and justice-seeking theologian stand out as a witness to 'the Jesus way' of full and flourishing life for all."

—**MICHAEL JAGESSAR**, independent researcher and writer

"This is a *cri de coeur* from a priest who has only ever wanted to be a prophetic voice for faith and inclusion. His indictment of the Unite Union as a 'cabal' fostering white privilege and imperialist ideology should give all faith workers pause and should also shame the leadership of the Church of England for the cultivation of secrecy and unaccountability in the face of complaint."

—**ANGELA TILBY**, canon emeritus, Christ Church Cathedral

To John

Faith in Unions

In Solidarity

David

Faith in Unions

Racism and Religious Exclusion in the Faith Workers
Branch of Unite the Union 2017–2020

David Isiorho

Foreword by Muhammad Al-Hussaini

RESOURCE *Publications* · Eugene, Oregon

FAITH IN UNIONS
Racism and Religious Exclusion in the Faith Workers Branch of Unite the Union
2017–2020

Resource Publications
An Imprint of Wipf and Stock Publishers
199 W. 8th Ave., Suite 3
Eugene, OR 97401

www.wipfandstock.com

PAPERBACK ISBN: 978-1-5326-9916-0
HARDCOVER ISBN: 978-1-5326-9917-7
EBOOK ISBN: 978-1-5326-9918-4

09/01/22

Faith in Unions is dedicated to the Cabal who control the Faith Workers branch of Unite the Union. My prayer is that they might reflect and re-think their direction of travel.

Faith in Unions is also dedicated to Len McCluskey, on whose watch as General Secretary of Unite the Union, the events recorded in this book took place. His support for me and the Faith Workers Branch was non-existent.

Finally, on a more positive note, I would like to thank my wife Linda, who listened patiently to my defiant anguish during those years when I was an active member of the Faith Worker's Branch. I appreciate her support and indorsement of this book.

Contents

Foreword

IT IS MY HONOUR to be appointed by The Reverend Dr David Isiorho and the Anglican Foundation, in the normal course of its business, for the purpose of contributing this foreword to his book on Church of England power politics relative to a multifaith clergy trades union.

As a courageous and prophetic Christian voice in Black Theology over decades, David has engaged these issues both from his deep scholarly knowledge and his lifelong personal path of racial struggle and suffering in obedience to the God who rules both conscience and righteous action. The total solidarity of David and his gracious wife, The Reverend Linda Isiorho, with injustices faced by victims of discrimination, abuse and bullying has been a rare example of uncompromising Christian integrity in the face of corrupt ecclesiastical power. They together have been a shining and godly teaching example in my little life.

My home is in the Irish-speaking Gaeltacht of County Donegal, whose vast green loveliness is redolent with the odour of the same English religious and racial oppression, echoed by the many souls of *An Gorta Mór*, the Great Hunger, which famine spirits still wander the derelict churches and cottages of this emptied land. In the townland of Ray outside Falcarragh, the eighth-century cross of St Colmcille stands fractured but resplendent within the ruins of the church. Here, in 1650, a platoon of Cromwell's Protestant soldiers burst in upon the Catholic congregation during Mass and slaughtered them in a massacre known as *Marfach Raithe*. Today's memorial sentinels which gaze westward over the Atlantic breakers testify to the mass emigration that was driven by such colonial genocide and starvation, in which the Church of the British Empire was at best passive onlooker, at worst active collaborator, as in so many other lands of occupation.

As I drive the twisting lanes by the mighty Blue Stack Mountains which cleave the county in two, the mist shrouding its highest peak, Croaghgorm, seems heavy with these generational tears of grief and sacrifice. Here for me is Ireland's Mount Moriah, where the majestic handiwork of the Creator collides with the inexplicable ruthlessness of God's demands upon his faithful children.

'Aqēdat Yītzhāq, the binding of Isaac upon the mountain in the land of Moriah, is narrated in Gen 22:1–19, and represents a pre-eminent and foundational scripture in Jewish belief, as well as in Islamic and Christian teaching. The eleventh-century rabbinical commentator, Shlōmō Yītzhāqī, known better by his acronym "Rashi", expounds this extraordinary passage.

In 22:1, pursuant to foregoing affairs: *ve-ha-Ēlōhīm nissāh et-Avrāhām*, "And God tested Abraham", wherein the root *n-s-h*, "to test, try", also connotes "to pull up", namely raising up Abraham to a higher spiritual level through this trial. God specifies fourfold in 22:2: *qach-nā et-binkhā et-yehīdekhā asher-āhavtā et-Yitzhāq*, "Please take your son, your only one, whom you love, Isaac", which Rashi identifies as divine assertions in the face of Abraham's repeated retorts that both Ishmael and Isaac are each "only son" of their respective mothers, and moreover that he loves them both. God shockingly requests Abraham to journey to Moriah: *ve-haʾālēhū shām le-ʿōlāh*, "And bring him up there as an offering", in which the root *ʿ-l-h* signifies "to go up, elevate, ascend" and applies both to the raising of Isaac upon the mountain and the whole burnt sacrifice that he is to become at the hand of his father. Rashi comments on this verse that God did not say to Abraham: *le-shachātō*, "to slaughter him", but rather: *le-haʾālōtō*, "to bring him up".

Both at 22:1, in God's call to Abraham, and 22:7, in Isaac's address to his father, the reply is: *hinnēnī*, "Here I am", which Rashi views as a response of piety and an expression of gentle humility in the face of such unimaginable horror. *Mōrīyāh* has resonance with the cognate Hebrew and Arabic roots for myrrh and bitterness, which in 22:12 stand as sentiments consubstantial with God's triumphant proclamation at the conclusion of the trial: *'attāh yādaʿtī kī-yerē Ēlōhīm attāh*, "Now I know that you are God-fearing".

The same story is referenced in *Quran* 37:100–108, where the son of Abraham is not named. In 37:101, the boy is described: *fa-bashsharnāhu bi-ghulāmin halīmin*, "We gave him tidings of a gentle lad". The ninth-century father of Islamic exegesis, Muhammad ibn Jarīr al-Tabarī, cites oral traditions of the companions of the Prophet Muhammad to identify the son, arguing that the gentle description of the boy as conveyed by the root *h-l-m* denoting "forebearance, longanimity", was an attribution to none except Isaac and Abraham.

In 37:102, Abraham declares that he has seen in a dream that he is to sacrifice his son, and asks him: *fa-ndhur mādhā tarā*, "So look you, what do you think?", to which the son replies: *if'al mā tu'maru satajidunī in sha' Allah min al-sābirīn*, "Do as you are commanded; you will find me, God willing, of the patient". The root *s-b-r* used here to describe Isaac's patience is held by the Arab lexicographers itself to connote "restraint, tying, confinement, withholding". In his commentary, al-Tabarī presents Isaac's words of utter obedience at the point of sacrifice, "Strengthen my bonds that I do not flounder, and avert from me your raiment that nothing of my blood spatters upon it, and Sarah sees it and grieves; and quicken the passing of the knife upon my neck lest I shame the death upon me". The Arabic cognate term to the Hebrew, *'aqīdah*, thus signifies both the tethering of the covenant upon Moriah, and the binding Islamic creed arising from God's holy writ.

In the New Testament, the Christological symbolism of the passage is evident, and Heb 11:17 states, *Pistei prosenēnochen Abraam ton Isaak peirazomenos*, "By faith Abraham offered up Isaac, being tested". Kierkegaard's characterisation of Abraham's actions as the zenith of faith in heaven's providence over human conscientious doubt is given in his term, "teleological suspension of the ethical". By contrast, rabbinical scholars such as the fourteenth-century exegete, Joseph Caspi, repudiated the suggestion that God could demand Abraham to commit such a deplorable act, which is also reflected in Buber's view, based on Hasidic precedents, that the actual test was for Abraham to overcome the inclination to obey God's command and act instead in godly love and compassion.

Disturbing, even disgusting, this Abrahamic paradigm of sacrifice in perfect vulnerable submission to suffering spans all three of the patriarch's daughter religions, and has been used and misused in every exemplar of heroic martyrdom and blind act of obedience to heaven's decree. At the same time, however, this story is the lived theology of victims of Shoah and genocide, persecuted minorities of belief and race, of survivors of sexual abuse in churches and faith-based institutions, and of every devout whistleblower-prophet exposing the godless wrongdoings within religious structures of power. The *'Aqēdah/'Aqīdah* binds us all in our sacrificial ordeal and our hopes of redemption.

What is clear in relation to the above is that the deep exploration and mining of our sacred texts for novel seams of meaning, precious gems of wisdom, has since early medieval times been at the heart of an enlivened intellectual conversation between Muslim and Jewish philologists of Quranic Arabic and biblical Hebrew. These were the architects of *exegesis traditionis*, the deep interpretation of Scripture through detailed linguistic analysis and under the authority of received oral traditions. Both Islamic *tafsir al-Qur'ān* and *sharh al-hadīth* as well as Judaic *midrāsh* and *gemara* study represent ancient and meticulously-crafted disciplines of interrogation of the written and oral revelation, with exegetical rules set by medieval scholars such as Ibn Hazm and Sa'adia Gaon.

What is important to recognise is that these traditions of wisdom reading are native and indigenous to their congregations of piety and learning, and are living and thriving praxes of dialectical small-group disputation around Scripture—such as Jewish *havrūtā-shī'ūr* study. While both Judaism and Islam are both houses splintered by internal sectarian division and strife, these varied intra-faith factions have each earned their right to authenticity, to legitimacy, by the longevity of the devotion of their followers and the jealous guardianship by their sages of these sacred exegetical practices which have been crafted and embedded over generations into the lifeblood of their communities of belief.

The modern interfaith industry, in the United Kingdom often dominated by leadership of the Church of England, is in many ways the very antithesis of Judaeo-Islamic attachment to deep communal scripturalism. For it could be argued that, from its Tudor inception, the Anglican relationship with religious truth has been shaped far less by habits of deep biblical study than by the power politics of holding together complex national institutions of monarchy, empire and church in the face of the people's deeply-held and sometimes conflicting Christian convictions. This so-called "Anglican Way", of old-boy network fudging of theological integrity in order to safeguard national or institutional unity, is to an outsider like me perhaps the CofE's most distinctive trademark.

In contrast to traditional Judaeo-Islamic communities of interpretation, the Anglo-Saxon Church is usually able to read the original Hebrew

Bible and Greek New Testament only in the King James English translation. It is a church whose pre-Christian beliefs in *Blut und Boden*, the "blood and soil" of English ethno-national destiny, synthesise uneasily with the foreign teachings of a darker-complexioned Palestinian rabbi. Between 1922 and 1945, the German Protestant churches openly sought to address this problem of race through the new theology of *Positives Christentum* or "Positive Christianity", remaking the Jewish Jesus as an Aryan antisemitic Christ-hero. *Positives Christentum* lives on powerfully in the muscular patriotism of the American megachurch, where sometimes I find it difficult to discern in the service where the cross ends and "The Star-Spangled Banner" begins. Equally, it finds expression in the Church of the British Empire's ceremonial alignment of God's will with the Crown's colonial policy and violence.

This reflects the essential problem of Western Christianity since the Constantinian conversion of 312, and the adoption of a dissenting Judaean sectarian movement of slaves and the poor as official state cult of pagan Roman Empire. With Palestinian Christianity's co-option over successive centuries into the apparatus of European kingly power, this resulted in its incongruous fusion with the warrior tribal religions which were already indigenous to the continent, and thereafter the enrolment of state terror to liquidate heterodox groups. The Western Church thus constitutes an ethnic pagan-Christian syncretism, whose dual ancestry finds expression Janus-like in congenital traits of scholarly Christian pietism and rapine Nordic conquest of inferior peoples—both these held concurrently.

The churches of the Anglosphere are thus veiled from the Aramaic Galilean world of *Yēshū'a/Yehōshū'a* by cumulative historical removes of Patristic Hellenisation, Imperial Romanisation, Protestant Germanisation, Tudor Anglicisation and industrial Americanisation, which expresses in white Protestant "patrician disdain" toward the alien, and concurrently a staggering lack of self-awareness as to its own un-Christian illegitimacy. As the borders of both Englishness and Anglicanism grew in the British Empire's expansion to continents of coloured races and non-Christian religions, scholars of Black Theology such as Isiorho and Reddie have commented how the Church of England emphatically became as much a signifier of white Anglo-Saxon normative identity as of Christianity. And from this, the theology emerged of the divinely-ordained mastership of Protestant Christian whiteness in the benign civilising mission to conquered peoples.

As was frankly asserted to me by a former Bishop of Winchester some years ago over dinner in Oxford, the global Anglican Communion is an outworking of Britain's colonising history. As such, he explained the candidature at that time of the Pakistani-origin Michael Nazir-Ali for appointment as Archbishop of Canterbury would be problematic for the African bishops who, in his view, would expect the man in the "top job", as he put it, to be of "English stock". The reality for black and Asian clergy of race prejudice and discrimination at the hands of both female and male officers within the Church of England has been extensively documented by Isiorho and others.

While most of England's former possessions are now sovereign and independent states in a Commonwealth of equals, the Anglican Communion appears in some instances not to have caught up with the idea. For in the celebrated description by Bishop Riah Hanna Abu El-Assal, Emeritus Anglican Bishop of Jerusalem, of Canon Guy Wilkinson as "the cancer at the heart of Anglicanism", is encapsulated a whole narrative of the venal culture and conduct of Church of England senior bureaucrats. I first encountered Wilkinson in his office as Secretary to the Archbishop of Canterbury for Inter-Religious Affairs in one of his controversial projects to create a state-funded Christian Muslim Forum under Lambeth Palace control.

When I started to raise concerns, shared both with Muslim and Christian colleagues of various denominations, I started to experience criminal harassment from Wilkinson for which the Metropolitan Police issued him with a Harassment Warning. I subsequently received reports from a diverse breadth of Catholic, United Reformed Church and Muslim clergy and lay colleagues of their parallel experiences of Wilkinson's expansive bullying and threats—misconduct that was truly ecumenical with testimonies of multiple victims. Bishop Riah's detailed account records how Wilkinson and Lambeth accomplices spared no ruthless effort to recolonise the Episcopal Church in Jerusalem and the Middle East and replace senior indigenous Palestinian clergy with ones approved by Head Office.

With Guy Wilkinson's public support for former prime minister, Tony Blair, in the latter's controversial attempts to enter the arena of inter-religious peace-making, it was inevitable that the imperialist hubris exhibited in the affairs of an overseas Anglican province would one day cross the red line into Church of England interference in the sovereign internal affairs of other religions. Thus, one of the most notorious instances of Church of England interfaith colonialism was the attempt several years ago by Guy Wilkinson and Lambeth Palace to disrupt an independent Anglo-American conference of rabbis and imams in the House of Lords, which the head of the rabbinic seminary where I was lecturing described as "appalling chutzpah by these Christians", and was met with defiance by the Jewish and Muslim clergy participants. In a notable and very oft-repeated tactic, when Wilkinson's bullying of the principal of the Jewish seminary did not achieve the desired outcome, he escalated the matter by going over the head of this professor to the trustees of this Jewish rabbinical college.

What is important to distil from the documentary evidence of this history is how the arrogance of religious-national imperialism, in this case white Anglican, generates for its perpetrators like Wilkinson both ruthlessness and sheer lack of any shame or boundaries in open violation of the autonomy of other communities of belief. And it is this paradigm of entitled bullying and violence for sake of defence of the institution that also speaks to the story of the Church of England's proxy colonialist interference in the multifaith clergy union, the Unite Faith Workers' Branch.

The Church of England's articulation with non-Christians is institutionally embodied in interfaith structures and appointment of dedicated bureaucrats, like Guy Wilkinson, within Lambeth Palace and Church House. The national Inter Faith Network for the United Kingdom (IFN) is a political-religious conglomeration of largely self-appointed "faith community representative bodies" and interfaith groups, which over the years has been funded in millions of pounds by the taxpayer and enjoys privileged lobbying access to government. Throughout its history, the IFN has been chaired by a largely static Church of England bishop or senior Anglican cleric, and a more frequently rotating non-Christian co-chair—invariably the important business of the Annual General Meeting is chaired by the Anglican co-chair. Since its creation by its lifetime salaried directors, Harriet Crabtree and Brian Pearce, the IFN has embodied the vested interests of a monetised interfaith industry and the project of the Church of England hierarchy to reinvent itself as a *primus inter pares* "head boy of Eton" for all UK faiths, just as England's bishops chase continued political relevance in the face of the CofE's own terminal decline in congregational numbers.

Satish Sharma, General Secretary of the National Council of Hindu Temples, bluntly describes the Inter Faith Network as being "From the outset a colonialist project to enforce and reinforce the ascendancy of the established Church of England over non-Christian faith communities in engagement with the British state. And in this, Crabtree and Pearce have acted as ruthless controlling agents and self-appointed gatekeepers". Sharma continues on to describe his experience of the Lambeth-sponsored

Hindu-Christian Forum as "Informed by a British Raj colonialism and thinly veiled racism, where liberal Church of England bishops handpick compliant Indian Anglophiles, and manipulate language of 'harmony' in order to tone police and impede honest debate. Behind the scenes, the Lambeth gatekeepers obstruct those Hindus who speak out and, in this, conservative black Christians are as much brothers in arms since they, like me, refuse to speak Anglican".

What is less immediately visible is the extent to which the controlling Crabtree-esque politics of these Anglican-led faith and interfaith organisations are realised through the systematic abuse and bullying of whistle-blowers, as a routine *modus operandi*. Sharma further writes that the Anglican IFN Executive Director, Harriet Crabtree, routinely interfered in internal Hindu community discussions around officer appointments, and how, despite his holding office as a Hindu trustee of the IFN, Crabtree refused to disclose to him correspondence that pertained to such alleged conduct by her.

When I myself publicly raised concerns on the record at the IFN Annual General Meeting about the membership within this government-funded charity of groups which were known to be linked to overseas Islamist organisations involved in genocide, it was Julian Bond, the Methodist Director of the Lambeth Palace-sponsored Christian Muslim Forum, who demanded that my remarks as a Muslim cleric about Islamist extremism be expunged from the minutes of the meeting. There followed a fraught correspondence in which the Anglican Executive Director of the IFN, Harriet Crabtree, and her colleagues stonewalled my insistence that my words be recorded truthfully and not censored.

And the whistle-blower's retribution for me means to this day, that every time I say, give a conference lecture or teach a scriptural seminar with my rabbi friend, Natan Levy, my clergy colleagues report to me on the record how Harriet Crabtree and other officials from the Inter Faith Network and beyond start phoning round and applying bullying pressure upon my academic and personal life.

In July 2019, when I wrote a doublet of articles in the *Church of England Newspaper* on the bullying of whistle-blowers of clergy abuse and malfeasance within Anglican, Muslim and interfaith bodies, this unleashed a tempest of political pressure from Church House upon the Unite Faith Workers' Branch, online smear from Peter Broadbent, a London suffragan bishop, and further harassing telephone calls to the newspaper from the former Lambeth Palace interfaith bureaucrat, Guy Wilkinson. Even my Jewish rabbi friend received calls to his workplace with threats around his organisational funding, simply because he and I work together.

My own interfaith trauma arose in the context of a project at St Ethelburga's Centre for Reconciliation and Peace in the Diocese of London of "Scriptural Reasoning" (SR), the practice of Jews, Christians and Muslims meeting to study their sacred books allegedly in order to foster a better quality of disagreement. This Quran and Bible study group at St Ethelburga's Centre was led by one William Campbell-Taylor (aka William Taylor), a Church of England vicar who had no knowledge of Biblical Hebrew or Classical Arabic, nor any fluency in New Testament Greek.

My first area of dismay was the inability of such Anglican leaders to engage at all original language biblical texts and traditions of interpretation, and my variously needing to dig deep into my fading schoolboy Greek to assist. David Ford, who claimed to be one of the "founder-leaders" of Scriptural Reasoning, I discovered in SR study sessions to have a poor knowledge of the Hebrew Bible and its native language and no education at all in Islamic Studies. The Jewish poet Haim Nachman Bialik's asseveration, "Reading the Bible in translation is like kissing your new bride through a veil", firmly embodies the centrality of Hebrew and Arabic grammar and philology in meaningful Judaeo-Islamic text study.

Pursuant to the foregoing, my second concern arose with what was Anglican-led SR's failure to respect indigenous ways of reading Islamic Scripture, namely alongside hadith and classical commentaries, which stand analogously to the rabbinic dialectical method. Among the controversial claims made by Scriptural Reasoning's Christian and Jewish founder figures is that of SR being a practice which challenges the binarism of modernist and fundamentalist approaches to religion by its re-engaging deep ancient traditions of sacred text study, in the pursuit of authenticity and novel shades of meaning.

American Jewish philosopher and SR co-founder, Peter Ochs, articulates this intention, "For the founders of Scriptural Reasoning, the original purpose was to repair what they judged to be inadequate academic methods for teaching scripture and scripturally-based religions, such as the Abrahamic religions". He asserts, "Many movements labeled 'fundamentalist' display tendencies to a modern Western-style binarism that has been written into the tissue of traditional religious practices and discourses". Ochs goes on to claim that Scriptural Reasoning "has not only the capacity, but also the authority to correct 'modernist reason'".

The counterfeit nature of this Fordian-Ochsian claim for SR's authority to correct extant interpretations of sacred texts through the engagement with ancient traditions of wisdom is vividly apparent in Anglican-led Scriptural Reasoning in the UK. Here, the hosting Church of England organisations that have co-opted SR for themselves and declare their personnel and their websites to be "official" are ones which have no *minhag/minhaj*, no timeless established Judaeo-Islamic discipline of dialectical *exegesis traditionis*, of thickly-reading holy books using instruments of philology, grammar, received oral tradition and sensitive exposition of concentric layers of literal through to allegorical readings of a verse.

Instead, Ford's Anglican-led SR becomes merely a poor kind of interfaith Protestant Bible study fashioned within the competency limitations of its self-appointed leadership, where ancient and subtle exegetical principles become supplanted by the one dominant hermeneutic of the Anglican-led interfaith industry and UK government community cohesion agenda.

Thus, thirdly, over time I became increasingly offended at the manipulation and instrumentalising of biblical and Quranic materials for political and funding agendas. Matters came to head when I discovered that the Director of St Etherburga's Centre had without my knowledge or my permission used Scriptural Reasoning text packs which I alone had prepared, with my own Arabic, Greek and Hebrew glosses and footnotes, as part of an application for thousands of pounds of government funding and salaries. For the record, no one has ever contested that the entirety of these resources were my work.

In my protesting such fraudulent behaviour with respect to sacred texts of God, I was instructed that, far from democratic parity of control in the project between the three participating faith houses, there was instead what David Ford claimed as "the asymmetries of hospitality" arising out of Anglican hosting and ownership in this initiative. This was followed up with the written proposal from St Ethelburga's that David Ford chair a "Scriptural Reasoning Reference Group" which would thereon exercise authority in relation to the proper usage and handling in SR of sacred Islamic and Jewish texts—matters which for centuries have been the sovereign and autonomous prerogative of jurists respectively of Islamic *sharīʿa* and Jewish *halakhāh* alone.

This scandal led Islamic authorities at Regent's Park Mosque to issue a *fatwā* on Scriptural Reasoning, demanding equality of the faiths round the table and prohibiting the use of *harām* or profane money in conjunction with sacred texts. While various ordinary SR participants from different faiths expressed solidarity with my blowing the whistle and/or began themselves to desert the group, I also started to receive threatening letters initiated by St Ethelburga's personnel.

As the colonialist outrages multiplied in this corrupt project, I began to discuss with other Christian and Jewish academics including my friends, Professor Kurt Anders Richardson, Professor Gareth Jones and others who had been present in the early meetings at the inception of Scriptural Reasoning at conferences of the American Academy of Religions. It was through these investigations that I learned of the history of cruel academic politics that had excluded Kurt, Gareth and other scholars in the beginnings of SR, and damaged their careers.

Over time, there emerged further bizarre Fordian manifestations of "invitation-only Scriptural Reasoning" meetings and even so-called "performance Scriptural Reasoning" of select SR grandees on a stage playing to an audience. These complemented David Ford's international SR roadshow events at the World Economic Forum and programmes for global politicians and monied sponsors. In a spirit evoking the builders of the Tower of Babel these represented for me a disturbing prostitution of sacred books of God for the profane egos of men and their material gain. The proposed collaboration by Ford's Cambridge Inter-Faith Programme with Tony Blair in the building of international Abraham House centres for the practice of SR among other things was in many ways a culmination of that profanity.

In a microcosm of much Church of England-led interfaith industry, Scriptural Reasoning's genesis is thus evidenced from an early juncture as a history of ungodly political manoeuvring and colonialist control. These are men, some of whom have neither textual scholarly *minhaj* or pedigree nor ethical reverence for the sanctity of sovereign religious traditions and their treasured holy books, just as surely as SR has been characterised by instances of financial dishonesty and victimisation of whistle-blowers. All of this taken together convicts some expressions of Scriptural Reasoning as *'amaliyya fāsida*, a "corrupt practice", which desecrates the very sanctity of what it purports to pursue in reverent study of Holy Writ.

In his celebrated essay, the Talmudist and theoretician, Joseph Soloveitchik, elaborates a biblical philosophical anthropology of three progressive levels of existential confrontation of humankind, and thereby articulates a rabbinical position on Jewish-Christian dialogue. While some have asserted that Soloveitchik's paper prohibits discussion by Jews with Christians other than on non-theological matters, in fact he asserts that dialogical encounter is one of subject-with-subject in parity of esteem and relationship, not subject-with-object after the Anglican "asymmetries of hospitality" model: "We shall resent any attempt on the part of the community of the many to engage us in a peculiar encounter in which our confronter will command us to take a position beneath him while placing himself not alongside of but above us . . . "We are not ready for a meeting with another faith community in which we shall become an object of observation, judgment and evaluation, even though the community of the many may then condescendingly display a sense of compassion with the community of the few and advise the many not to harm or persecute the few".

The Catholic theologian, Michel Schooyans, offers a withering critique of the attempt by certain World Economic Forum interfaith globalists like Blair to encroach upon the sovereignty of Christian doctrine: "This project threatens to set us back to an age in which political power was ascribed the mission of promoting a religious confession, or of changing it. In the case of the Tony Blair Faith Foundation, this is also a matter of promoting one and only one religious confession, which a universal, global political power would impose on the entire world".

Furthermore, the Church of England has been rocked by scandals of sexual abuse, nationally unmasked in damning reports of the Independent Inquiry into Child Sexual Abuse (IICSA), the Elliot Review and the Gibb Report into vulnerable adult abuse. Yet concurrently with Archbishop Justin Welby's televised expressions of tearful regret, the Bishop of London, Sarah Mullally, and other leaders of the Church of England continue to employ scandal management companies such as Luther Pendragon Limited, which malignant entity also undertakes reputation management for the tobacco industry, the arms industry and the nuclear waste industry.

Luther Pendragon has been implicated in the cover-up of Anglican sexual abuse as well as scandal management of other malfeasance within the Church of England, and was summoned by the parliamentary Public Administration Select Committee for its refusal to come under regulation of the Association of Professional Political Consultants. In July 2015, I met in a delegation of leading abuse survivors with Justin Welby at Lambeth Palace to raise our concerns about the Bishop of London's determined use of this company to threaten and disrupt a parliamentary meeting on clergy abuse.

In surveying this history of the behaviour of officers in the Church of England, the events related by Isiorho in his narrative of the Unite Faith Workers' Branch should thus be lucid and fully consonant with all we have come to learn about the organisational culture that frames the established church. In 2020, the national press reported extensively how Steven Saxby, Anglican vicar and Chair of the Unite Faith Workers' Branch and Officer of Church of England Clergy Advocates (CECA), was suspended as a candidate for the Labour Party for alleged sexual harassment, and further dismissed in disgrace by the Church for repeated adultery. National organisations for survivors of clergy sexual abuse have expressed the most grave concern at the harmful positions adopted by CECA relative to reform of the Clergy Discipline Measure 2003.

In conclusion, I can only raise up in prayer the providence of heaven in opening the heart of readers to David's courageous and honest exposition, and that honesty and truth may prevail in the wake of such persecution and suffering.

Sheikh Dr Muhammad Al-Hussaini
Senior Lecturer in Islamic Studies at the Oxford
Centre for Religion and Public Life

Introduction

Banbury, Brede and Bristol

I RECENTLY EXCHANGED STRAPLINES with a colleague who was clearly coming at the Christian faith from a different direction to me. This colleague said that it was about *'Searching for God's heart; sharing what we find'*. I did not disagree with him as I actually thought it was rather good although not particularly original as I had heard something like this before. However, when I suggested a strapline that went a bit deeper and more theological, he did that very English thing which is to shy away from anything intellectual, branding it as somehow highbrow and too difficult to deal with. Another colleague uses Mic 6:8. *"What does the Lord require of you but to do justice, and to love kindness, and to walk humbly with your God?"* This clearly has a lot more going for it as it suggests a closeness to God rather than a fishing trip to find the divine nature. There really is milage in following the *be still and know that I am God* approach.

My own strapline is *Ministry Together Rooted in Christ: Promoting Contextual and Practical Theology*. So, my understanding of Mission is what we do and the theology of mission is the way we talk about God and our part in glad service. To rediscover the Gospel here in the UK we need to reconsider our context. Mission England of the Billy Graham era is over and so is the decade of evangelism in the run-up to the millennium. Faith in the City and Faith in the Countryside are part of our history but not working documents for change any more, if they ever were. Our context is now characterised by uncertainty as we try to theologise the full consequences

1

of a post Brexit and pandemic world. So, where do we go from here? How do we regain the Christ model for ourselves in our contemporary context? We start with a realisation that we must rediscover the catholicity of the universal Church. For the Church of England that means we must re-imaging ourselves as part of an international fellowship. Furthermore, it means giving renewed focus to our parish system where most of the faithful reside.

It is interesting how everything in the Church of England suddenly became mission-shaped. However, this re-imaging has not included race, gender and equality issues. God is great and finds all kinds of ways to communicate with us. Yet, each one of us has our own tolerances and our own ways of being that need to be respected. In *The Acts of the Apostles*, Luke made it very clear that the kingdom depends upon the active participation of all with all the diversity of talents and ministries that this involves. Bringing people deeper into faith usually means giving them more opportunities to minister in their own unique ways.

My theology is inclusive; my life experience has taught me this. As a boy in the sixties, born to a White mother and a Black father who then divorced; as a child dubbed 'thick' due to my unrecognised dyslexia and dyspraxia; as someone who knew his brain worked with a sense of having a mission to express the inexhaustible love of God—long sentence for long experience—I learned to my bones how precious we each are.

In the Diocese of Truro, I was a member of the Diversity and Equality Committee, an ecumenical group of Anglicans and Methodists from across Cornwall with a passion to promote inclusion within our churches and chapels. We produced a diocesan leaflet called WELCOMING ALL GOD'S PEOPLE—A SIMPLE GUIDE. In that publication, we sought to emphasise that we are all God's people and that each one of us is made in the image of God, redeemed in the blood of Christ. As Christians, we believe God is the creator of all humanity and that Jesus showed us how, as his disciples, we should be welcoming of all, whatever their origin, situation and condition. We should discriminate against none. Jesus spent time with all kinds of people and welcomed them as children of God. Our thinking here was that all are included and welcomed not only because we are disciples of Christ, but also because as UK citizens, we seek to abide by the legislative requirements of our country.

So how do we go about rediscovering the Gospel here in Britain? All people must be treated fairly and equally. The Church must acknowledge that equality and diversity legislation culminating in the Equality Act of

2010 which sought to remove discrimination, marginalisation and exclusion. Sadly, we acknowledge that prejudices do exist in our communities. As we follow Christ's command to 'Love one another as I have loved you', we have the great opportunity to take the lead in being fully inclusive and welcoming, working to eliminate discrimination and to change attitudes.

So, what about recruitment and retention of those working for a faith organisation? I feel an integral part of my testimony and witness includes using myself as a case study. We start with recruitment to faith worker responsibilities in the Church of England. What follows are three very brief case studies of posts I have applied for in recent years, two bog-standard parish jobs, and a middle management responsibility. These applications are the contexts in which clergy, particularly Black clergy, seek deployment and if employed reach their glass ceiling very quickly. This is all fertile ground for trade union membership.

Banbury St Mary's is a town-centre parish which prides itself on being inclusive and a promotor of equality. So, I started my application by commending them for their position on justice issues pointing out that I personally perceive the institution of the Church of England as a place seriously lacking in that regard. I have applied for too many posts where my skills and experience have been overlooked in favour of White candidates whose appointment favours a church that excludes people. I am not embittered by my experiences but rather focused on truth and justice for our Lord. I wanted them to know that I was a dynamic person who wants to embrace the inclusion problematic and to move things on.

I passionately believe in the equality of the Christian gospel and am very willing to work collaboratively with anyone who feels the same. On their wish list they were looking for a lively confident speaker. Over the years I have addressed a number of audiences on a variety of topics from quiet 8 o'clock Book of Common Prayer services, to small groups observing the Stations of the Cross, to lecture halls full of students, to packed cathedrals. Work with universities and with The Queen's Foundation had called upon my academic skills, both here and in The Netherlands at Vrije Universiteit, Amsterdam, working with doctoral students. I have served a number of different parishes with a very wide range of people. As a sociologist and a Black theologian, I am curious and interested in who and how people are. As a priest, I seek to discern the *imago dei,* the image of God, in all.

Banbury had identified a number of areas of ministry to shape its life and work. I believed I could build on this and maintain the momentum for further growth. I have worked in seven dioceses in very different parishes. In addition to working with congregations whose average age is sixty-five and ministering to nursing homes and all ages in between, I would come to this process with my own track record of working with young people and leading parishes to growth. I felt that, given the stressing of inclusivity, having membership of inclusive Church Network, emphasis on the arts (particularly music), that I would be a good fit and was almost certainly guaranteed to be short listed.

So, what went wrong? According to the letter from the bishop involved there were eight other candidates and he was sorry to say that the panel decided not to short-list me for interview. Well, would I really expect to be interviewed with such a strong numerical field? I was then advised to contact the bishop's PA to arrange a mutually convenient time to talk and provide detailed feedback on my application. I booked an appointment with the bishop's secretary for 12:00 noon a few days later. I duly phoned and the secretary explained that the bishop was away from the office. He would call back which he did about quarter of an hour later. To be fair, he was very apologetic and did give a reasonable explanation but it had set a tone.

What follows now are notes from a telephone conversation I had with the bishop. The bishop went on to explain that there had been nine applications—well, ten actually, but the tenth was not in Holy Orders. He added that this one was a difficult one in terms of deciding who to call in. He further recognised that I was experienced with many strengths which he correctly identified, proving at least that he had read the application. The bishop then began to focus on my ecclesiology, putting me at the Anglo Catholic end of the spectrum, which, incidentally, is not how I describe myself. The matter of ecclesiology had not been particularly a feature of either the job spec or of my application, though I had noted that vestments appeared in many of the pictures provided in the profile which does not smack of a 'middling' style of worship, his term, but broadly modern catholic. I concluded later that they had got this information about me from elsewhere which raises a number of questions, not least those of confidentiality and protocol.

This is my deduction and may well not be the case but that is what I have arrived at. The bishop several times referred to this parish as being 'middling' as opposed to another church in the area, which was high, information I did not need and could not locate in any context. The bishop said that in the end they shortlisted four candidates 'more in line with where the parish is at.' He went on to detail how the selected candidates fitted the diversity and inclusivity agenda: a candidate he initially referred to as BME, not BAME, before correcting himself; one with serious disabilities, he hesitated over choosing the qualifier here; there were two female candidates and two males because 'they did want to be inclusive.' At which point, I queried how inclusive they were if they were unable to select a modern catholic priest. There was a short silence, then, with a tone of surprise, 'Oh, I see what you mean.' He concluded that there was 'nothing in particular' he could pick out for specific guidance on the application as 'it was fine.' I mildly pointed out that this was the third advertisement for this post at which point the bishop saw his opportunity to close a conversation that he was evidently not enjoying, and, to be fair, these are difficult talks to have, so he said it was indeed and they would be grateful for my prayers and bade farewell.

The issue of ecclesiology is an interesting one. In all my applications I say the following by way of clarification: *Raised as an Anglican, within the Anglo-Catholic tradition, I now describe myself as Church of England, liberal, reformed and Catholic.* If I needed a label, I would describe myself as a sacramentalist who is comfortable with a modern Catholic worship style.

The second case study involved an application for a basic grade job where I was the only candidate. On this occasion I did get an interview presumably because I was the only priest interested in the position. So why did I want to be Rector of Brede, Udimore, Beckley and Peasmarsh? It was a rural high church situation and I believed that I met the criterion of the job description and person specification and therefore could fulfil this role effectively.

When I read the parish profile, I was very drawn to this position. I could locate many of their expressed needs within my experience. As my application evinced, I had served in a wide range of parishes from inner city, where we must understand deprivation, to rural shires, where the challenges of ministry to rich people presents itself. I find myself excited by the possibilities for growth, especially the use of occasional offices as a platform for mission. So, I had been drawn in prayer to making this application to be Rector of Brede, Udimore, Beckley and Peasmarsh. I very much wanted to work with these congregations in making sense of their commitment to church growth as we would seek in partnership to progress the kingdom. Crucial to this will be building and implementing a shared vision plan for lay ministry.

• • •

I am a pastor working within the liberal catholic tradition who believes people should feel cared for and cherished. At the heart of any ministry is pastoral care for all age groups within the parish: ready to lead, to follow, to comfort or afflict, to walk beside people in barren days and to celebrate alongside in times of richness, to visit and care at all times. I also believe that ministry is about priests enabling and skilling lay people to find their own ministries, those good works prepared for them to walk in.

I have a proven record for leading parishes to growth with many years' experience in parochial ministry. I am a person of prayerful and entrepreneurial vigour, with a desire to see the renewal and equipping of congregations and plant in the service of God. An important part of this would be a visible and outward-looking presence in the villages of this benefice. I also believe I am a person with pastoral sensitivity and emotional intelligence. I have gained experience in the provision of a wide range of pastoral care. I believe that strong communication skills are essential. I would bring to this my formal qualifications in psychology and sociology, knowing that listening skills are key to successful interaction and to the development of productive discourses. I am a trained counsellor and social group worker. Incidentally, the Diploma in Applications of Psychology qualifies me as a negotiator, a formal skill pertinent to working in teams and groups.

I wanted the interviewers to know that beauty in worship and varied preaching are important to me. A keen musician and singer myself, I understand how sound enriches worship. I love the use of multisensory adornments that the catholic tradition embraces. One size does not fit all; I am ready to lead various styles of liturgies as appropriate. I also value the mission opportunities presented by the occasional offices. Anything that can bring the Kingdom nearer to people is precious. Firmly in the central catholic tradition of the Anglican church I feel strongly that worship should offer people a variety of languages that put their minds towards God, and the register and the spectacle are important. In other words, to comfort and to proclaim are the keynotes of my praxis.

I wanted those interviewing me to believe I have an engaging decision-making style. This is evidenced by my belief that the Vicar's ministry is the meeting point of the ministry of the whole parish. I am a proven manager who can provide sound leadership yet work collaboratively as part of a team ministry to continue the growth and development of the life of the church. I would seek to lead, encourage, and develop existing and new ordained and lay ministries. I believe I have the ability successfully to lead a team of people in a church or secular context. I believe I have good time management skills. My working style is to be ahead of deadlines. I also believe I have a proven ability to work collaboratively to discern vision and values, and to work strategically to implement them. Being a member of a Trinitarian faith bespeaks an understanding of teamwork and collaboration. If God does not operate in a unitary fashion, then why should we? Teams challenge and support and extend the work of all involved, bringing greater creativity within a context of mutual trust. In previous parishes I had worked with a team of retired clergy and readers. I continued to evince my commitment to working collaboratively. As they would have seen from my application I have worked in several situations where delegation has been vital to call upon all the skills available to achieve the goal. I am not a one-man show and never have been and do not relish the prospect of becoming one. I see leadership as nurture, coming from a pastoral perspective always. What can you effect on your own—truly little that lasts.

Archdeacon Edward Dowler who chaired the interview panel along with one of the parish representative gave me some instant but brief feedback before I left the benefice. They were not going to appoint me because the answers I gave to their questions were too diffuse. It is interesting he did not use the words 'vague' or 'irrelevant' although that was clearly the context of his argument. The linguistically cautious archdeacon would write to me when he returned from his holiday with more detailed feedback. During this meeting the parish representative refused to look at me. I have come across this in other interview situations.[1]

The feedback was as follows. The Parochial Church Council representatives and other members of the panel very much warmed to me as a person and as a priest, finding me a gentle and kind personality with whom they would enjoy working, and having day-to-day contact as their parish priest. They were also of course impressed by my theological background and record of publication. However, they were concerned by a lack of specific contextual reference to the parish profile and the particular challenges

1. I was interviewed for the post of Mission Priest, at St Mary & St Eanswythe with St Saviour, Folkestone in the Diocese of Canterbury on 3rd July 2019. During the presentation I gave, one of the Churchwardens refused to make eye contact with me. There was clearly an atmosphere in the room which I believe came from him. As a parish representative he had the power of veto and he knew it. I was not appointed even though everybody else I had met warmed to me and were looking forward to my ministry among them. There were no other candidates. As part of the interview process at East Grinstead (3rd May 2016) the person conducting the tour of the Vicarage would not look at me and addressed all communications exclusively to my white wife.

facing the benefice. The general comment was that my answers, although always engaging, were somewhat diffuse and so it was difficult for them to see with very much precision how I would be likely to approach the task. For example, my answer on church growth concentrated very much on work with children and families, and did not reflect on outreach to older age groups, who are in many ways the most prominent groups in the villages. This must be the first time in my ministry that a parish has said to me that only limited focus should be given to young families and schools. What was being said here was contrary to what they wrote in their profile. The panel would also have been grateful to hear more about my current work, also in a rural or (as they understood it) semi-rural benefice. They had heard about my completion of various building/repair projects—all of which was reassuring in a benefice with several grade-1 listed buildings—but they claimed they did not hear very much about other aspects of the pastoral and mission work I had undertaken as a priest in Cornwall. So, did they not read my application or hear what I said in response to their questions on pastoral care?

On the safeguarding question which took the form of a hypothetical situation, the archdeacon said it would perhaps have been helpful if I had made it clear that I would have made some kind of written record of what had been said by the person who had approached me about a potential abuse situation so that this could be transmitted to the Diocesan Safeguarding Adviser. This is interesting because if I had not made a written record in such a situation how could I have communicated my concerns with the safeguarding officer in any professional way? Why should I have to state the obvious to these people? Just how stupid did they think I was? Do they treat all candidates this way? It could be argued that it is best not to over investigate during the initial stages of a disclosure as leading questions can distort the evidence. If I had emphasised my note-taking, I am sure their complaint would have been just that. I probably know a lot more about safeguarding than this archdeacon.[2] The game that was being played here is to nit-pick on every detail to justify their decision not to appoint me to this benefice and perhaps convince even themselves that they were being fair. On the particular historic situation in Brede, the Archdeacon claimed it would have been helpful also to have had some rather more specific suggestions from me about how I might reach out to those who are still affected by the actions of a

2. I was appointed Priest-In-Charge of St Michael, Brereton, in 1993 and followed an incumbent who had been convicted and imprisoned for child abuse.

previous incumbent who had abused children, for example by visiting those who continue to be especially hurt or concerned. I made it very clear at the interview that I was coming to this process with considerable experience of how to follow an incumbent who had abused children and the pastoral work that it entailed. I am beginning to wonder if the archdeacon had really listened to anything I had to say. Chichester Diocese does not have a good record on dealing with abuse which may explain why they in this context are projecting their failures on to me.[3] Clearly, the interview panel and Parochial Church Council representatives were not ready for a Black Rector at Brede, Udimore, Beckley and Peasmarsh. As far as I am concerned the issues raised in the feedback were lies to cover up their racism.

This brings us to my third case study. In February 2019 I applied for the Black job in the Diocese of Bristol. The role description identified the Dean for Black and Minority Ethnic Ministry as an educational and theological lead within the parishes of St Agnes and St Anne's and across the diocese. As a Black priest who received national coverage when becoming the first Black vicar in Handsworth, my work has been a marker of a healing and consoling presence of a deeply pastoral kind. This has helped me to understand what a ministry of being means through the way that my presence has helped many people to gain their own voice. I also feel that this has completed a journey of enrichment for me that would allow me to operate on a bigger scale beyond the parish boundaries in the wider Church and world.

Handsworth, St James, is in an inner-city area, poor, with high rates of transience and greater levels of poverty and unemployment than most other parts of the country. Its very name, Handsworth, became notoriously associated with riots. The area is calmer now due to investment in material and social resources. How long that may endure in the present economic climate remains to be seen. This is a very religious area, crammed with churches of all kinds, mosques, gurdwaras and mandirs, yet there is almost a village feel to the place. Along with responsibility for the pastoral care of St. James', I also acted as Pastoral Lead and Consultant Minister for the Good News Asian Church. An associate priest was licensed to take

3. At East Grinstead (3rd May 2016) I was not appointed. Concern was raised by the Archdeacon that I was the default Safe Guarding Officer in my then-present post in Birmingham, an intercity area where people were not keen to take on such responsibilities. It was felt that this role should have been taken up by a lay person and that somehow it was my fault that they didn't. This is rich coming from a Diocese which was under investigation at the time for alleged cover-up of child abuse.

responsibility for the day-to-day running of this proprietary chapel whilst I retained oversight. Good News Asian Church was the first independent Asian church in the country. It uses a range of liturgies and languages, proud and very aware of the Indian heritage of two thousand years of Christianity. Another well-established link with the wider community was the Grove Project which provides a range of high-quality childcare activities including nursery provision, wrap around care, holiday play schemes as well as training for parents and carers. I was chair of this project and acted as line manager for the project co-ordinator. We employed twelve members of staff. This team was a crucial part of parish outreach work.

I passionately believe in the equality agenda expressed through the Christian gospel and am very willing to work collaboratively with anyone who feels the same. I had just published a book on inclusion with Wipf and Stock Publishers—*Mission, Anguish, and Defiance: A Personal Experience of Black Clergy Deployment in the Church of England*. At the time of my application, I had been invited to speak at the USPG international conference in March 2020—Re-thinking Mission: Rediscovering the Gospel in 'Christian' Nations in 2020 which I was looking forward to.

The role of dean for Black and ethnic minority ministry is not a role to be lightly undertaken but is one that would best be done by someone who can combine significant parish experience with academic integrity. My sense of vocation embraces all aspects of my person, intellectually, aesthetically, emotionally and spiritually. I am a practical theologian with considerable and varied experience of lifelong learning and would like to share that richness within the context of this role. I believed I would be credible in the post.

I was indeed offered an interview for the post of priest-in-charge of St Agnes and St Anne's and Dean for Black and Minority Ethnic Ministry. However, within days it was decided to postpone the interviews to keep everyone safe during the pandemic. They appreciated my disappointment but I should be assured that they were delighted with my application and wanted to see me as soon as it was practicable. In the coming weeks the Diocese would produce a contingency plan for an interview. They would remain committed to a robust and equitable recruitment methodology even if compromises had to be made on the regular process. So, the HR speak went.

A few weeks later I had another email this time from archdeacon Neil thanking me again for my patience about the postponement of the interview and letting me know that the Bishop's staff team were committed to progressing this appointment and filling the role. They now wanted to explore an alternative to a face-to-face interview and wondered if I would be prepared to be interviewed by the panel via Zoom? The idea here was to discern a preferred candidate using Zoom so that a preliminary offer could be made.

I responded to the Archdeacon by saying that I fully realise that these are truly remarkable times and that the usual processes and procedures are constantly in flux. I can talk HR as good as the next person. It is good to be reassured that they were keen, as a diocese, to progress this appointment. I was very willing to be interviewed via Zoom and to accept the outlines that had been suggested. Like many others, the zeitgeist and technology are meeting in some unexpected ways that we do well to profit from. More HR from me. The Archdeacon thanked me for getting back to him and being willing to proceed this way and that he would be in touch again in the next week with further details when he had heard from all candidates. As it turned out not everyone on the panel were willing to progress this via Zoom, so that didn't happen. In the meantime, I was thanked again for my patience. It was becoming clearer to me that the bishop's staff meeting did not know how to make this appointment. Eventually the archdeacon wrote saying they wanted to be open and honest with me. When an email starts like that you just know it is not going to be beneficial for you as the recipient. The archdeacon had met with the panel and following many conversations with the bishop about the role they decided that it was only fair to all concerned to take the very difficult decision to stop the current recruitment process at this time. They needed to take this time to evaluate the situation, so that they could offer me the essential clarity required when considering a new role. They are so considerate. You see, they were still looking forward to meeting me but not quite yet. The idea now was to give all the parties sometime in the coming months to decide how they would manage the needs of this role. The archdeacon would be in touch with me as things became clearer as to where they were going with this post. The important thing was that they would like me to re-apply for this post. They would be happy to use my previously submitted application form, or I would be welcome to update it and send it again. What a shambals. How seriously could they expect me to take this? I should have just walked away from these incompetent people and shaken the dust off my sandals but I decided to go along with it and see where it went.

The next episode in this saga was to inform me that the role had now been changed. What a surprise. As the archdeacon explained, the tragic death of George Floyd, the Black Lives Matter movement and the toppling of the Colston statue led the bishop to make a statement on her determination to bring racial justice to Bristol Diocese. Are these people for real. In short, the bishop now needed immediate support in that work and time to consider potential roles in the diocese related to racial justice. It was decided to separate the Dean of BAME Ministry from the parish post at St Agnes and St Anne's. So, someone was asked to fulfil the racial justice role on an interim basis. Well, if they were so keen on my application why did they not ask the Bishop of Truro to release me for that crucial and immediate work?

Well, the plans of the bishop's staff group were moved forward as they intended to re-advertise and interview in the autumn purely for the post of priest-in-Charge of St Agnes and St Anne's. I was told that this remains a significant and substantial role and it's likely the appointee will be involved in the wider work on racial justice if appropriate. The archdeacon did appreciate that these changes mean I would need to reflect and discern afresh. I did reflect on this, withdrew my application and was appointed to a post in another Diocese. I had waited nearly a year for this post to come to interview but as it turned out I was led in a different direction. I asked HR to pass on my warmest regards to Archdeacon Neil with whom I have had several interesting conversations about this post.

This case study and the previous two represent clearly defined contexts in which trade union intervention might be profitable in challenging institutionalised racism. It is very difficult for Black clergy who are seen as the *other* to secure employment in the Church of England. Even when they are well established, they find barriers to their progression to new parish situations, let alone anything that looks like promotion. The next section of the introduction considers what role if any trade unions can play when the focus moves from recruitment to retention of Faith Workers' condition of service.

So, what is the reality check on Trade Unions? The story of a Faith Workers' Branch goes back to the days when we were a clergy section within the finance and manufacturing union which was launched on Thursday 15th September 1994. It began with fifteen members and soon grew to several hundred. Even in those days it was not exclusively Anglican and the organisation was open to faith workers from all denominations and faiths. It was particularly attractive to those suffering injustice at the hands of a Faith employer. Then MSF became Amicus, which merged with Unite and its clergy section became the Faith Workers' Branch.

Introduction

During the triennial of 2017–2020 I was secretary of the national branch of the Faith Workers' Union. During that time, I had the privilege of talking with many Union members about why they had joined. A lot of the members got involved as a response to concerns they had about job security. Members felt that they needed support legally and emotionally, in order to fight their corner and serve the people they ministered to. There was talk about the importance of union representation in the light of diocesan policies and under the new climate of ministry in the Church of England whose legal structure is known as Common Tenure. Some had seen clergy friends who had suffered unfair complaints from churchwardens. There was a feeling that faith organisations had become more managerial but had inadequate HR staff with legal knowledge and authority. Furthermore, boundaries were very unclear and that faith workers were being mistreated. A very strong reason for joining Unite was to stay connected with other faith workers so that we can build our strength and unity against injustice. Some people do join for purely ideological reasons and agree with the socialist principles which should undergird it. Clearly if you are on the left in politics, you are likely to think that unions are a good thing and should be supported.

What members liked about the union included knowing that work was being done in support of individual members who were being bullied by church authorities and that members who were subject to disciplinary action were supported by union representatives. It was reported that there had been a prompt response from the branch helpline and that those at the end of the phone seem committed, engaged and knowledgeable. It was commented that you know you can call the helpline at any time and it gives you a sense of security. On occasion I did ask members what would lead them to resign their membership. I asked directly about what actions or policy endorsed by the branch or unite might lead them to resign their membership? The general feeling was anything that encouraged division or mistrust between faiths or denominations would be grounds for resignation. Furthermore, any action or policy that limited or withdrew the rights of any group or policies that were anti-LGBT, anti-feminist or racist would not be acceptable to the membership. Some members also felt that it would be a concern to them if the branch started to seem too Anglican.

The first chapter of this book focuses on my own story as a parish priest who was on the receiving end of racialised discrimination in the Diocese of Truro. I consider union intervention in Cornwall which gives support to why clergy and those who work for a faith organisation would want to join a trade union. Having left the Diocese of Truro our discussion moves on to the wider work of the Faith Workers' Branch and its relationship to the parent body Unite the Union. So, what about the trade union value of Equality? On 16th July 2018 the Faith Workers' Branch Executive Committee of Unite the Union received an equalities report with priorities for the next three years. This was the only detailed report given to the branch during the triennial. An explicit aim for the recent branch elections was to increase diversity on the Executive Committee. A minimum of five places for women was set and achieved. For the first time, in fact, 50 percent of the executives were now female, including two out of five officers. Denominationally, we came from the Anglican, Methodist, Roman Catholic and Jewish traditions. One immediate task facing the new Executive Committee was to assess the extent to which they reflected the membership of the branch in terms such as regional, racial, denominational and LGBT representation. A major concern was support for same-sex couples. The exemptions for faith organisations from same-sex marriage legislation causes problems for many of our members. The Executive Committee recently issued a statement in support of the decision of the Scottish Episcopal Church to offer same-sex marriage. Another focus was an age-compulsory retirement for the Church of England clergy at seventy. Several cases had arisen in the branch over this issue. It is no longer legal for most employers to set an age of retirement but there are exemptions. This had been brought to the attention of the Executive Committee for ongoing assessment.

We learnt from the report that the branch did not keep records on the faith affiliation of members as this is not required information on joining the union and that the largest single membership group is Church of England clergy, followed by Methodist ministers. So clearly work needed to be done on identifying who the membership were but it was far from clear how this was to be progressed. At the branch meeting in April 2019, it was reported that the general secretary was planning to have a meeting with the rabbis that had left Unite following complaints they had made about Antisemitism. The General Secretary's office has been in touch with a renewed invitation to our former members to meet with him to discuss the issue of antisemitism within the Labour Party and the union movement. It was suggested that another possibility might be to arrange a seminar meeting, to which current members, especially rabbis, but also including other Jewish members of Unite, could be invited to share ideas for resolving the issue. A check on the union database had revealed several rabbis listed within other branches of Unite and they were being advised that they were eligible to join our branch.

The April Executive Committee discussed membership among different faith communities and how we could encourage greater take up. According to its standing orders the Executive Committee had the power to co-opt up to four further members in order to assist in establishing a gender balance and to be mindful of the under-representation of BAME and LGBT people and the desirability of appropriate representation from the branch's recognised workplace sub-groups. On the agenda was the co-options of a prominent rabbi to the Executive Committee. It was decided not to co-op the rabbi but rather to encourage him to stand when a position became vacant. The tone of the discussion was offensive. It was even suggested that since we already had one rabbi, we did not need another. I pointed out to my colleges that this is how White people discuss Black appointments. This was not the only occasion when Anglican and Methodists had joined forces to prevent co-options. Muhammad Al-Hussaini had proposed that a Hindu member be co-opted on to the Executive Committee. The acting chair refused to put this to the vote on the grounds that she had received advice from unite officials that we should circulate the membership over co-options.

At a meeting in January 2019, Mohamed Al-Hussaini put forward an agenda item on the branch's possible input and consultation with the independent inquiry into child sexual abuse. The chair and legal team of the inquiry were seeking advice from faith-based organisations in relation to child protection and safeguarding systems of religious institutions in England and Wales. The idea here was to build a dialogue with groups like Faith Workers in respect of issues of safeguarding, bullying and abuse of power in faith settings. The Executive Committee authorised Muhammad Al-Hussaini to enter into a conversation with officials from the inquiry to explore the branch's involvement. The legal counsel for the independent inquiry had approached the branch seeking data about our experience of safeguarding issues and bullying of clergy who have been whistle-blowers of abuses. By the time of our next meeting, Anglican and Methodist members of the Executive Committee had decided they did not want Muhammad Al-Hussaini to represent them on this body so the branch was unable to make a decision on applying for Core Participant status. This was the beginning of a very spiteful campaign against the only muslin member of the Executive Committee. From then on, every agenda item Muhammad Al-Hussaini put forwarded would be opposed if not vetoed by this group.

I wrote to the General Secretary to inform him of my current concerns and to seek his advice. I wanted our leader to know that as a branch we have been traversing choppy seas of late with our chair, The Revd Canon Stephen Trott, stepping down over what he called 'a vendetta' against Muhammad Al-Hussaini, an eminent theologian and member of our Executive Committee. Muhammad Al-Hussaini had informed us of the forthcoming publication of two articles about institutionalised religion and sexual abuse which would be in The Church of England Newspaper. The Executive Committee broadly applauded him and approved of what he had written. Muhammad referred to himself as a member of the Faith Workers' Branch but nowhere did he even remotely claim to be a representative of or as speaking on behalf of anyone but himself. Next thing I knew was that a disclaimer on the articles had been published. This purported to be an official complaint issued by the branch but it was not. I was given to understand that the branch treasurer had approached the *Church of England Newspaper* despite not being authorised to do so by the Executive Committee. I informed the General Secretary that the on-going fall out will be managed by us internally but to my mind this was heavy handed and unnecessary. The treasurer had taken this course of action against the advice of the chair and without talking to me as branch secretary but with the full cooperation of the London regional officer. This officer advised me not to seek any mediation in this matter. This was not advice but rather direction and when I did not fully comply with her wishes I was accused of a lack of judgement in the rudest of tones. I have been a trade unionist all my working life and am better qualified than most people in our movement. I don't expect to be treated as if I was stupid. I concluded my communication by assuring the general secretary of my full co-operation with the enquiry that was likely to follow a formal complaint. Readers will not be surprised to hear that I did not receive a reply.

In July 2020 I presented a report to the Executive Committee of the Faith Workers' Branch which clearly challenged the union for being White and exclusive in its approach. What do I mean by this? From the start, I should say that, as an Anglican, I find myself critical of my own tradition, because I am very familiar with its foibles and idiosyncrasies, and this will sometimes involve using polemic to challenge its senior leadership. My critique is motivated by a genuine love of the Church of England because I care deeply about this organisation. I am writing as an insider, as a priest and baptised member, and as an outsider as a member of the Black and minority ethnic category. The killing of George Floyd reflects the daily injustices that Black people face and that includes the things that take place in Unite the Union. My report takes the form of a litany of concern and theological reflection on the work of the committee structure of the Faith Workers' branch.

When meetings are chaired in such a way that points of order are ruled against before they have been heard: **Does Unite have its knee on the neck of its Black members?** When agenda items are not discussed and even deleted by the acting chair following last-minute discussions with Unite officials: **Does Unite have its knee on the neck of its Black members?** When we are denied faith-based workplace groupings other than Christian: **Does Unite have its knee on the neck of its Black members?** When able people from faiths other than Christian are denied membership of our Executive Committee: **Does Unite have its knee on the neck of its Black members?** When the branch secretary is told by the acting chair to rewrite the minutes of the previous meeting before their circulation: **Does Unite have its knee on the neck of its Black members?** When branch officers conspire to organise private meetings with unite officials without the branch secretary: **Does Unite have its knee on the neck of its Black members?** When clearly defined roles in the Unite Rule book for the branch secretary are usurped by the acting chair with the agreement of Unite officials: **Does Unite have its knee on the neck of its Black members?** When Unite officials invite lawyers to agenda setting meetings: **Does Unite have its knee on the neck of its Black members?** When the branch secretary has no confidence in Unite officials not to undermine his position and side with other officers within the branch against him: **Does Unite have its knee on the neck of its Black members?** When the branch secretary is falsely accused of not consulting the chair when draft agenda has been tabled many weeks in advance: **Does Unite have its knee on the neck of its Black members?** When so little has been done to address the equality issues facing the Faith Workers' Branch: **Does Unite have its knee on the neck of its Black members?** When the branch secretary is Black: **Does Unite have its knee on the neck of its Black members.**

The Faith Workers' Executive Committee is dominated by Anglicans and Methodist who control the ethos of the branch. There has been collusion between Executive Committee members and Unite officers who have excluded the contributions of other faith groups. Furthermore, it is likely that senior Anglican officials have been able to influence the decisions of the union through consultations with branch officers. On 8th August 2021 I resigned my membership of the Unite Union. This comes after nearly thirty years of membership and nearly a decade serving on the Branch Executive Committee. I stood down as secretary at the beginning of that year. Seven months on a complaint was levelled against me in which I was accused of the promoting a direct attack on the Faith Workers' Branch in a public arena. This very broad allegation was made without any evidence to support it. I don't know who made the complaint within Unite, perhaps we will never find out. My response was to quit such an organisation and to make it perfectly clear, that I refute any allegations of wrong doing. I thought I was allowed to express a difference of opinion, to speak out against injustice and whistle blow discrimination as I experienced it. I have been growingly concerned about the casual disregard for the equal treatment of members. Clearly union members think that Unite is in support of unions values and promotes equality. That the membership has an automatic right to legal support if something goes wrong with their terms of their employment. But what if I were to tell them on both accounts that this is just not true. In the Unite Rulebook, it is clearly stated that inclusivity is a core value. I have personally witnessed discrimination in action and have suffered from it myself. I have been a senior shop steward for this organisation and know that members rarely get legal representation when they are dismissed or made redundant. Now, to have unfounded accusations flung at me brings my union journey with Unite to an end. I had completely lost faith in the Faith Workers' Branch and would no longer jeopardise my integrity by remaining associated with it. The reasons why I left Unite are the subject matter of this book.

This introduction sets out the context in which people are recruited into the Faith Workers' Union. Chapter 1 gives some focus to retention of Black faith worker deployment in the Church of England through the lens of my own case study. This book has things to say about discriminatory practices which puts the discussion about Englishness and Britishness into a wider context. *Faith in Unions* is concerned with the difficulty of doing theology in a White faith context. Chapter 2 gives critique to the idea of a single British identity and is initiated by a likely direction for travel of the faith workers in the next twenty-five years. Chapter 3 gives focus to Muslim and Hindu workplace groupings within the Faith Workers' Branch and the opposition to their formation from Anglican and Methodist Christian members. This chapter is concerned with the struggle for faith recognition within a discriminatory and institutionally racist Union structure. I am suggesting a political agenda associated with English ethnicity as the mode of involvement to explain plans in the Faith Workers' Branch that are likely to result in further religious exclusion. Chapter 4 is a theoretical chapter that revisits the immigrant host relationships model between the indigenous White English population and so-called newcomers who are a racialised other. This chapter is an explicit exploration of what I mean by the term 'racialised' other in the context of the British Labour movement. In this we need to understand the ways historical Christianity has defined Black identities. I have deliberately used seminal works which were contemporary to the time to avoid too many reconstructions of past events. My conclusion starts a wider discussion of English exclusivity and a signpost to antisemitism and Islamophobia.

Chapter One

Why Join a Trade Union

DURING THE FIRST COVID lockdown I was accused of neglecting my clergical duties while I was parish priest for Charles Town, Par and Tywardreath in the Diocese of Truro. I have been in ministry now for over thirty years and I am very accustomed to dealing with people who present with difficulties, because that is how the job comes. I knew I needed a thick shirt and a thick skin for Anglican ministry. However, I must say that this was the first time I have been accused of being invisible and not pulling my weight. The complaint had been made to the archdeacon during a Zoom conversation she had had with my churchwardens. I really do not understand why they did not come to me directly with their issues. We may not have agreed upon everything but at least then we would have known what each other was feeling and would have been able to explore the common ground. The churchwardens had concerns about the time I was giving to research work and union matters. What could they possibly know about how I manage my time? Clearly, they would have liked to have line managed me and controlled me. Maybe they just thought they could do my job of overseeing three parishes and five churches better than I did. A reference was made to a preschool group as an outreach opportunity that I had failed to perceive. I had only been invited to Little Lambs on one occasion, but I cannot see how my regular attendance there could be considered part of my priestly duties especially as the woman leading this is highly skilled. I would not want her to think I was interfering or questioning her competence. In Birmingham, I line managed a nursery with twelve full-time members of staff, but nobody expected me to attend any of the classes. As clergy, we must tread a fine balance of freeing laity to do those good works given for them to do whilst providing back up if it is required.

Despite the claim that I was neglecting my parochial responsibilities a considerable number of emails were exchanged which I have kept as evidence of my engagement. Emails sent to me were often the vehicle of complaint. A good example of this is as follows from the churchwarden at Tywardreath which read as follows—

> I have received several comments from members of our congregation and others, wondering what you are doing in terms of pastoral duties in the present situation. The extract below is fairly typical of such comments. I know I'm not the only one thinking it but has anyone asked Fr David why he isn't doing anything. Most of the other clergy in the area are online streaming services or at least sermons. At such an unprecedented time like this we need spiritual guidance and ours is decidedly lacking. It really isn't good enough is it? Sorry to rant. I know it's not your fault but the rest of us are ringing around checking on our congregation, fetching shopping, prescriptions etc. What is he doing? His excuse is his wife is over 70 but so are most of us.

The churchwarden asked me to give him some guidance on how to respond. I advised him to nip this in the bud quite quickly. He really needed to tell these people and others that things were in place in all the parishes in terms of using social media to help people to keep in touch with each other during the pandemic. The start of a weekly vicar's message during the coronavirus crisis had been sent out and put on the Church of England webpages—*A Church Near You*. My contribution to the cancelled Lent course also appears here. I was working with Charlestown for the weekly message to go on YouTube and to be available to all parishes. Furthermore, I had plans to livestream a service on Easter Day from the parsonage. I told the Tywardeath churchwarden that if the people making these complaints don't accept his response based on my advice, then to please refer them directly to me for spiritual direction. I concluded my email correspondence by reminding him that this was only day 2 of a lockdown that could continue for weeks.

There was no acknowledgement that this was a fast-evolving situation, by the way, with every member of the parochial clergy playing catchup with their ICT skills. I had no response from the Tywardeath churchwarden, so

I followed up with a phone call which was not received. Not deterred by this, I wrote a formal letter sent through the post to him which was also not acknowledged or addressed in any way. I do not see what else I could have done. I had a conversation with the Tywardeath churchwarden on the eve of lockdown as he had been phoning around to get support for cancelling the annual meeting which was due after the 11:00 am communion service. I agreed to this request then I found out the following morning that he had not informed the church secretary who turned up with all the paper work required for such a meeting. She was particularly distressed because her husband was in a vulnerable category and she feared endangering him. I apologised for what had happen.

On Good Friday I made a video of the Prayer Book Communion service to be used on Easter Sunday. It took all day to produce. I received some uninvited feedback from the churchwarden at Par, headed "Take two required please!" The email was as follows—

> It just does not portray the image of the major Christian Festival it is supposed to represent. The setting is all wrong. . . . Please use the dining room table, with a clear background, perhaps a wall with a couple of pictures on it. With a larger table you would have room to put all the books you require, alongside the sacraments and a couple of candles. Take one reminds me of you being 'set up' in the middle of a book fair! A short Easter message would be encouraging, don't you think? especially in the present predicament,[sic] we are all in. Apologies if this appears ungrateful but I'm not happy with this being released, representing you and the parishes of which you serve.

This communication was invasive and oppositional with no grasp of how difficult it can be to use equipment that is not up to the job. I could have ordered video resources of various kinds, but this would have been expensive and who would have paid for it? So how do you respond to such a cruel email. My wife and I don't usually work together but on this occasion, we did join forces to produce this online service. We did not ask for their feedback but we did expect their appreciation of the considerable effort that went into producing the video. We did the best we could in our small and inadequate vicarage. Linda sent an email explaining we were both very upset by their response and we asked the churchwarden to reflect on her harshness on this holy day to a priest who was doing his best to remain faithful at this difficult time.

On 21 June 2020 I appeared on *Sunday Morning Live*, the BBC religious affairs programme talking about the legacy of slavery. There were complaints to and from churchwardens. Archdeacon Audrey said that some disquiet had been expressed about the language and responses I gave. Churchwardens had to respond to a number of expressions of shock and concern from within their communities. They questioned the appropriateness of a priest appearing to condone vandalism and challenge to church authorities. However, the Bishop of Truro made it noticeably clear that he had little sympathy with anyone complaining about my appearance on *Sunday Live*. I was, in his opinion, entirely within my rights to appear and to contribute as I did. It did cause a lot of discussion; comments to me, unsurprisingly, were very positive but the usual group of malcontents, who, incidentally, never came to church if I was there apparently did not like this, and neither did they like my recently published book, *Mission Anguish and Defiance: A Personal Experience of Black Clergy Deployment in the Church of England*. I wonder if they realise what image this gives of their inner life.

• • •

The start of lockdown and the partial lifting of lockdown have raised anxiety levels nationally and locally which is all very understandable. The lockdown has also emphasised that there is little effective co-working across these three diverse and quite different parishes. For example, Linda and I attended as many social events as we could, clearly before lockdown. We frequently found that Par would be organizing a bazaar on the same Saturday that Tywardreath was putting on a soup and sweet lunch. This caused us some considerable time juggling! I also supported events that the churchwardens in Par would not support such as my regular attendance at Mother's Union meetings and the men's breakfast. With respect to a wider profile, I ensured that there is where humanly possible a "Thought for the Day" style article in the local paper, *St Austell Voice*, coordinating this and seeking to include as many people as possible, both clergy and lay. As you can imagine, this involved considerable time and effort on my part. No churchwarden has ever acknowledged this but there has been much feedback from appreciative readers.

I think Archdeacon Audrey was right about there being something of a collective perception between the churchwardens, but my question is why? I have been trying to get these folks to work together—not that they have, by turning on me. I realise that these are strange times but, given their queries, why have they cancelled all the joint services? I guess the psychology behind it is the panic that appears to be driving certainly the government's agenda at the time. The whole business of masking is so strange to us that it is bound to induce fear. Maybe this has affected the churchwardens who expect their earthly father to do what our heavenly Father is apparently not doing, i.e., zapping the virus. There is a steady stream of scholarly literature emerging to deal with this issue—when I find time to read it all and pray about it.

Reconciliation involves the acknowledgement of all parties that there is a matter to be resolved. The principles of restorative justice can help here but I suspect the churchwardens would not accept that as it would involve them acknowledging their own neediness, a process that accusation would preclude. I think we need to understand each parish separately, remembering that we did not know how representative these views were amongst regular church members. I invited Archdeacon Audrey to come to each parish to preach about the central role of reconciliation in Christianity. She declined.

Disciplinary Action

During lockdown I was confined to barracks by the Diocese of Truro. However, this did not prevent Bishop Phillip and Archdeacon Audrey from giving support to people who claimed I was neglecting my duties. I was accused of not providing pastoral support through remote means. This has caused considerable distress to Linda, my wife, and myself and we felt very hurt and betrayed by the churchwardens in this matter. I have an evidence trail of numerous emails, phone calls, Zoom meetings, and various publications that speak otherwise. In some respects, I had been busier than ever, it feels. And why now? Three months after lockdown? Perhaps this is some form of collective and panicky agoraphobia; there has been much talk of the emotional challenges coming out of lockdown. As a psychologist, I am naturally very interested in such processes.

I did not have an underlying health condition which prevented me from exercising public ministry but my wife was over seventy and suffered from brittle asthma. I was told by Bishop Phillip not to conduct weddings and funerals services in to order to protect her. Following government guidance, he was now quite rightly including ministers who lived with someone in a vulnerable category. However, there was a blatant contradiction in what was being said to me and about me. It was appreciated that at the bishop's direction I had to remove myself from public ministry to protect Linda. At the same time there was a shared perception on the part of the Churchwardens about my alleged "absence" from the life of the parishes, resulting in my failure to provide guidance and help for the churches during this period of lockdown. It is amazing how White people can face two ways at the same time. It is a variant of speaking with a forked tongue.

At a meeting with Archdeacon Audrey, I was invited to talk about how I had spent the first three months of lockdown. I had been involved in prayer, getting to grips with new technologies, phoning people including churchwardens, a Mother's Union person and pastoral coordinator from Par, various other people from all three parishes, and ill and bereaved people. I had already sent Archdeacon Audrey a three-page document providing detailed evidence of pastoral emails and phone calls. I wanted on the record my efforts to provide supervision of those engaged in pastoral work within the parishes albeit via remote means. I wanted some acknowledgement that I had tried to communicate with churchwardens to check out how they were managing their roles and responsibilities, and above all to offer them support. Archdeacon Audrey indicated that she had no intention in the context of this meeting to go through the details of what had or had not been said and done—rather this was about looking at the bigger picture. I asked if my document had been shared with the churchwardens. I was told that it had not been shared with them because of not wanting to get into the minute details at this stage.

So, I then asked if this was a formal or disciplinary meeting. At this stage in the conversation a whole new set of contradictions kicked in. It was not a disciplinary meeting as the diocese would like to keep it informal, and find a positive way forward without having to resort to any formal processes. However, Archdeacon Audrey indicated that there were grounds for taking seriously the concerns that had been expressed and that she also wanted me to be aware that they were not entirely surprised by the concerns, because informal feedback in the past had indicated that all was not well in the parishes. This was supported by Bishop Phillip whose understanding was that the wardens have significant concerns that must be addressed in one way or another. This felt like a disciplinary meeting to me. Union experience tells us that if it feels like a disciplinary it probably is. So here I was, the Branch Secretary of the Faith Workers' Union in an unofficial disciplinary situation on trial in a kangaroo court. The judge and jury were a very unpleasant archdeacon who was aware that I was applying for a number of posts elsewhere in the country, but assured me that nothing about this had be revealed to anyone in the parishes. Why would an archdeacon need to say that given that a breach of confidentiality is a serious matter and could result in dismissal even for senior staff. I indicated that my reason for applying for new posts, even within the diocese, was out of a desire to have a new challenge at this stage in my ministry, not because I was in any way unhappy in my current position. Clearly the situation had changed after these allegations but I would have been unwise to say that during this undefined meeting.

Archdeacon Audrey suggested that a way forward, for the sake of my ministry, and for the sake of the life of the respective churches, would be to establish a process of mediation between me and my estranged churchwardens using professional mediators. I was obliged to go with this at least to the point of finding out how they would affect mediation. Bridge Builders would be the organisation which would be used to provide the mediation. However, I wanted to know details regarding the people and the process so that I could feel safe and comfortable within it.

I was informed that the usual process was that the lead mediator and a colleague would have a meeting with each individual separately first (probably about one to two hours) then this is followed by a longer joint meeting with all parties. The joint meeting would only happen if all parties agree to it, and if Bridge Builders feels that mediation would be beneficial. I was told that mediation will give all parties their opportunity to explain in detail the situation as they understood it. The meeting ended with Archdeacon Audrey reminding me that the aim was to find a way to enable my ministry to flourish, and the life of all churches to flourish too. I didn't believe a word that was said. I had to accept this mediation or face a formal disciplinary procedure. Readers should note that one of the churchwardens stated on record that she did not wish to be part of a disciplinary process which could result in the vicar losing his job. So, it was clear to me what was being planned by the three churchwardens who would participate in this process and the archdeacon.

So how did each churchwarden find themselves in a conversation with the archdeacon and with each other to talk about their perception of me during lockdown? Did they meet with each other prior to their meeting with the archdeacon and if so, who initiated it and why? Or were they all invited into the conversation by the archdeacon given that Zoom meetings require a host? To respond prayerfully to their concerns, I needed to know how this conversation started. I do know that a few days before I received Archdeacon Audrey's email, I had been in conversation with her and churchwardens at Par concerning the difficulty of meeting Common Fund requirements. Furthermore, the archdeacon intended to contact those wardens about this. I told the churchwardens at Par and Tywardreath that I had a Zoom meeting with Archdeacon Audrey about another matter and if there were any concerns, they wanted me to raise, I would be happy to do so.

The churchwardens contacted the archdeacon following my appearance on *Sunday Morning Live* on 21 June regarding Black Lives Matter. So clearly this was a major part of their complaint. According to Archdeacon Audrey's notes, the broadcast and lockdown together have brought to a head the concerns which have been felt about my ministry from the beginning. They were shocked by the challenge I made to the Church of England hierarchy and by comments about cheering statue destruction, and my wife spitting on the same. My book didn't go down too well and was understood as the outburst of an angry writer, and demonstrated unresolved issues for me and Linda. Clearly racism is a major factor and an effective mediation process would need to acknowledge this. Linda was puzzled if not annoyed that she was mentioned, as we do not work together formally, liturgically, or pastorally, although she tries to support at social events, tedious though they may be.

So, this all started with the publication of my book and appearance on *Sunday Morning Live*. Clearly my new status as an author and my appearance on a respected and balanced television programme had affected them. The churchwardens would be at pains to point out that their concerns had no racial undertones. I would need to confront them on this otherwise there will be no basis for discussion. I did try to speak with them prior to mediation but they were not responsive to a meaningful discussion. These were people with things to hide so they went into defense mode and denial.

Clearly there were a lot of questions to be asked before any meaningful conversation could possibly take place with the churchwardens. The fundamental question was, is this situation one that will lend itself to mediation anyway? What is the viability of the whole project? I wanted the churchwardens to recognise the difficulties I faced with three parishes and five worship centres and no curate. They presumably wanted me to work full-time in each parish. I do know of priests who try to do this, give up their day off, holidays, retreats, and quiet time, and work into the early hours of the morning. I came across a clergy person a few years ago who was faced with a similar situation to mine who ended up with early retirement following his collapse at a funeral. I have promised my wife that I am not willing to do that, as it is bad stewardship.

So, what did I want from this process if it were to go as far as a conversation with churchwardens? I would want them to know that their accusation, of my 'absence' from the life of the parishes during lockdown, has caused considerable distress to Linda and myself and we feel very hurt and betrayed by them in this matter. I think the mediators should have asked them if they want me gone from the parochial situation at Charlestown, Par, and Tywardreath, as certainly the tone of notes with the archdeacon would suggest this.

> 'Why is he here?' 'Is the context really the right one for him?' 'No great opportunities for social justice.'

I have never heard them use this kind of language. The churchwarden at Tywardreath was very clear in his communication with the archdeacon that he wanted me to be dismissed because I was the cause of all the parishes' problems. He seemed to think that the diocese would provide some kind of interim minister to put things right. Where did he get that idea from?

I wrote to Bridge Builders to clarify with them a number of issues, not least their credential for doing this work. According to the bishop they came very highly recommended, were highly professional, and were there to enable mediation and reconciliation and certainly not to take sides. It all sounded a bit to good to be true, so I checked it out for myself and found them wanting on a number of accounts. I had a number of questions for the so-called professional mediators. I asked them directly what exactly were their qualifications for this kind of work given that I could not find a CV on their website. What professional associations do they belong to? What was their track record and where are the testimonials from people they have assisted? What experience do they have in dealing with people of colour, especially as I had identified several overt expressions of racism in what the churchwardens were saying and doing? So, what types of mediation techniques did they most use and what might be their plan to utilise when dealing with my situation? I wanted to know why they appeared to be ignoring the information I had sent them? Were they aware and sensitive to the subtleties of the ecclesiology of people who define themselves as liberal catholic? And how will they address the apparent narrowness of vision, the small world that the churchwardens appear to be inhabiting?

The Bridge Builders mediation process bore little resemblance to other tried and tested approaches to conflict management. The mediation process seemed to me a strange one. They wanted me supported by a silent witness in the background to enter a conversation with three other people who were in conflict with him. A discussion then was to take place without any mediation between the participants prior to when they meet in the joint meeting. The role of the mediator here seemed to be more akin to that of a counsellor which was fine if the leaders had the professional accreditation to do such work and the situation warranted it. I would need some convincing as to whether Bridge Builders were able to resolve this type of conflict in that sort of way. Their documentation was lacking in that respect. They did not want a report but advocated agreements between parties to which they will provide some follow-up. I did not know how this would fit with my conditions of service as a church office holder or as a member of the Faith Branch of the Unite Union, who would have to be consulted about such a contact with churchwardens given that churchwardens are not my employers or line managers. The whole thing was completely half-baked on their part. Furthermore, I could not see how a meeting conducted via Zoom would be genuinely viable. There were plenty of spaces around where socially distanced meetings could have been held.

Union Action

I wrote to Bishop Phillip acknowledging that his archdeacon was to invite me to a meeting as part of the Diocesan complaints policy following the breakdown of the mediation offered by Bridge Builders. So, a formal procedure was now on the table as a result of my failure to participate in an informal and voluntary process. I made it perfectly clear to the bishop that I felt that I was being victimised by Archdeacon Audrey. My wife, Linda, wrote a limerick.[1] I had explored the Bridge Builders' offer and found it unacceptable to me as a way forward largely because they refused to provide me with their credentials as mediators. I also had concerns about what they meant by confidentiality, and shared this with them. Now I suddenly found myself in what I can only describe as a disciplinary meeting and was told that there was still time to avoid this more formal process by returning to Bridge Builders. According to the bishop the opportunity of working with

---

1. There was an Archdeacon called Audrey whose intellect was drab and ordinary. Her pastoral care made Hitler look fair which rendered her ministry tawdry.

them was an invitation and refusing it does not mean that the issues go away. The idea of suggesting Bridge Builders was to enable that to happen in as positive an environment as possible. I perceived this as bullying, and it was stressful to endure. Clearly not a voluntary option.

I now told Bishop Phillip that I had made arrangements for union representation at this proposed meeting at the end of September, but I wondered if the Diocese of Turo really wanted to pursue this in the way it had been suggested. Given that churchwardens are bishops' officers, would not a frank conversation between them and the bishop be more productive as a way forward? After all, at this stage there was no breakdown of relationship with churchwardens, and if anything, things have been cordial as always, if not openly friendly. I reminded the bishop that I had been looking for a move and that I had secured an interview with another diocese. I concluded my email by saying that I would appreciate the space now to explore that and other options and hopefully leave Cornwall without further unpleasantness.

So, it was time to call in the union, but clearly, I could not represent myself in this matter. My union representative was my friend and colleague Muhammad Al-Hussaini. Fortunately, the person co-ordinating the Faith Workers' helpline was also a friend who strongly advised that we seek to take the archdeacon out of this process as she was clearly hostile towards me as evidenced by her willingness to have a meeting with my churchwardens without me and about me. I forwarded to Muhammad Al-Hussaini the communications I had from the bishop and archdeacon and asked that he now take charge of communications with them. Muhammad Al-Hussaini wrote to the bishop and archdeacon as the appointed union representative acting on my behalf. He explained that he was an accredited workplace representative of the Unite Faith Workers' Branch on its Executive Committee. He also wanted them to know that he was a regional representative on the Unite National Black, Asian and Ethnic Minority Committee, having a particular concern for the interests of Black clergy in the Church of England and other faith settings. In the opening correspondence it would become clear to the bishop and archdeacon that Muhammad Al-Hussaini was very familiar with national Church of England processes pertaining to clergy discipline, canon law, and guidelines for clergy professional conduct. However, for completeness he asked them if they would kindly furnish him with the diocesan complaints procedures and materials concerning clergy standards. On this they directed him to their website.

Muhammad Al-Hussaini confirmed that I was fully supportive of an independently-facilitated mediation process in order to address and resolve the issues that have been raised. The union advice here is that all parties agree on an independent professional mediator which does not have links with the Church of England hierarchy. Furthermore, the union was pleased to explore and offer suggestions of suitable organisations in this respect. Muhammad Al-Hussaini concluded his email by saying that he was confident that through the auspices of a mutually agreed and wholly independent mediator, the issues in the parish can be discussed and resolved.

Muhammad Al-Hussaini had to wait for an acknowledgment of his correspondence as his email had gone into the junk boxes of both the bishop and the archdeacon. He approached them again to initiate a discussion of the engagement of a mutually agreed-on and appropriate mediation body. Eventually we had a response saying that they were pleased that I was open to mediation. We were pleased that a line of communication had at last been established with the hope that all parties could agree on an independent professional mediation body which could take matters forward and resolve issues in the best interests of all. The union recommend the Centre for Effective Dispute Resolution (CEDR) as a highly-regarded mediation body, with which I was happy as to its independence. Muhammad Al-Hussaini concluded his correspondence by asking for their thoughts, and expressed his desire to work together in advancing the mediation process. Clearly concerns flow in both directions, and any mediation process would need to be established under as neutral parameters as possible. This would need to acknowledge not just the concerns of churchwardens but include my response to what they had to say and also my concerns about the pattern of victimisation I had experienced from them and by the archdeacon. The wider context would need to acknowledge institutional racism within the Church of England.

At this point Bishop Phillip became defensive and acknowledged the serious nature of the allegation that had been made against his archdeacon. I had the usual pious email that included his greetings to me and Linda, and that he appreciated how hard this must be for us. The bishop was quite sure this is not a situation any of us wanted, least of all the archdeacon. The bishop would now reply to all communications and was doing so with the archdeacon's agreement. So, perhaps Bishop Phillip had rediscovered his spine and decided to take charge of the situation, something I had been asking him to do for some time? However, the style of communications had changed and it was clear to me that lawyers and HR were now the script writers, if not the whole senior management team giving support to this new and unsure bishop. Emails now had headings. Issues about my ministry and accusations against the archdeacon would be dealt with separately. The HR person had been asked to contact the Centre for Effective Dispute Resolution (CEDR) and advise the bishop on their appropriateness for these circumstances. If we agree to use them, HR will contact the church-wardens and see if they are still willing to engage in a mediated process.

As for allegation of victimisation the bishop was very concerned about this. Until this matter was resolved it was decided that the alternative archdeacon from the neighboring archdeaconry takes on responsibility as my archdeacon. The bishop thought this was a sensible and non-judgmental action. Many others saw it as admission of guilt on the part of the Diocese. Muhammad Al-Hussaini responded to the latest round of correspondence and could confirm that I was grateful for the oversight of a different archdeacon as a practical arrangement, and requested that this arrangement continued indefinitely.

So, what was to stop me from bring a complaint against Archdeacon Audrey through the Diocese own complaints procedures? I did consider this but realised I would have to bring a complaint against Bishop Phillip also. The Diocesan complaints procedure had already been seriously compromised by the recorded response of the bishop to me, when he wrote to express his concerns, namely the bishop stating *prima facie* that he could not believe that Archdeacon Audrey would victimise me. I believe his words to me were along the lines that no one has any desire to victimise me in any way, but rather to address the issues in as cordial and professional a way as possible. More to the point, I really had no confidence in church complaints procedures. These procedures were not going to work in my favour against those in position of authority over me. I had been caused considerable distress and alarm by these events and the institutional response of the diocese.

Union officers had discussed this history and recent correspondence, and it was noted with some concern that HR did not appear to have offered support to me in this situation, though they were open to correction if this was not the case. The Union had the clear impression that Bishop Phillip, Diocesan authorities, and HR had prioritised institutional advocacy and support for an archdeacon, rather than demonstrating equal and fair support for both parties in this dispute. The whole matter was handled poorly and unkindly from the outset, causing significant unnecessary suffering to several people. I therefore welcomed the intervention of the bishop in his assignment of a different archdeacon and requested that this arrangement remain in place until such time as I leave the diocese. I did leave the Diocese of Turo and was able to draw a line under my ordeal. I wiped the excrement off my shoes and moved on. For a more refined and focused response you need to read the Mission of the Seventy Disciples and consider the woes to unrepentant cities in St Luke's Gospel.[2]

2. Luke 10:1–16.

Chapter Two

The Single British Identity
inherited from New Labour

THIS CHAPTER STARTS WITH a consideration of the contemporary direction of travel for the Faith Worker Branch, its hopes and aspirations for future trade union work. This leads to a realisation that this vision does not include Muslim and Hindu union members who voices are marginalised and lost in the adoption of a single British identity favored by a dominant Church of England and Methodist culture. The model is one of an immigrant-host relationship in which anything which is not White or Christian will be subordinated to the dominant ethos. Like trickle-down economics, other faiths are said to benefit in the long term from this approach because what is good for the White Christian majority is in the best interests of all. This is very much a history chapter giving focus to Englishness as a dominant culture within a notion of Britishness as seen through an account of Robert Runcie's leadership of the Church of England. Drawing upon Humphrey Carpenter's biography, an attempt is made to put the Runcie Archiepiscopate into its very English context during the years in which Mrs Thatcher was prime minister. I consider areas of conflict between church and state including the Falklands Memorial Service. However, the idea that the Church of England and the Thatcher regime were constantly at loggerheads is firmly rejected. Runcie's belief in establishment is presented by Carpenter as very much to do with state occasions, being on first-name terms with members of the government, attending posh parties. Thus, the archbishop comes across as neither overtly political nor spiritual. Carpenter apportions considerably more space in the biography to the royal family than to inner cities even though Runcie is associated in the media with support for urban projects. The chapter concludes with the post-Runcie era of modern conservative known as the Big Society.

Union Campaigns and Their Direction of Travel

In July 2019 the Faith Workers' Branch celebrated twenty-five years of its life as a trade union branch. Arising from that meeting the acting chair, Ruth Oates, and treasurer, Pete Hobson, had two follow-up meetings with Gail Carmail, the assistant General Secretary, Siobhan Endean, national officer and also Nicole Charlett, who was the Faith-Workers-designated union officer from the London and East Region. These meetings were set up without my knowledge or approval as branch secretary. Adrian Judd, the branch's training officer, reassured me that I was not been excluded from this process and Terry Yong, the helpline coordinator could not understand what I was making a fuss about when I raised an objection as to the way these meeting were convened. If they were an informal part of a genuine training programme then I would have been happy for them to go ahead as planned. As it turned out I was right to ask that they be put on hold until I could attend. There had been too many misunderstandings of late in the Faith Workers' Branch and I really wanted to avoid any further unpleasantness. I was initially told that these meetings were informal and part of our ongoing training programme. The meetings went ahead without me and became the springboard for a major clarification of focus for the Faith Workers' Branch.

At the first meeting of the Faith Workers' Cabal[1] as I am going to call it, they revisited the Branch's history, both long-term and more recent, and it was clear they wanted to centre the branch exclusively on the needs of Anglican clergy and lay workers. This took place on 31st October 2019 and they met again on 29th November to set out a range of options that could be brought to the Executive Committee for further discussion. They disregarded the wide variety of faith-based contexts our members work in. They

---

1. The Cabal is defined as an unaccountable fraction who engages in political intrigue to promote a definite set of objectives internal to their own problematic. I am using the term to describe the actions of union officials who make oligarch decisions as conspiracy, collusion, conniving, and scheming.

wanted to demonstrate that over half our members were Church of England clergy with a significant number more being lay employees of the Church of England. So, the advice was to use this as a primary lens through which to focus our organizing and campaigning efforts. Clearly, they could only do this by neglecting work in other faith contexts where a critical mass of members was also present. It was therefore suggested that we look to build on the significant success over recent years in our relationships with the Church of England hierarchy, in the belief that this strategy could be resourced by Unite. They proposed a survey of all our members to justify this approach or as they put it to clarify our priorities for our activity in the next few years. This group wanted more recognition from the Church of England, the Methodist Church, and the Unitarian Free Church for trade union work as this would support and protect Christian members. They also prioritised further Christian workplace groupings, in particular in the United Reform Church. There was an agenda item on doing more work with the Unite database to get a better understanding of how our members are recorded. Another interesting topic for discussion without the branch secretary.

The direction of travel in the Faith Workers' Branch is very much in line with a post-colonial understanding of Britishness and the integration of faiths other than Christian and cultures into the dominant ethos. There are Muslim and Hindu faith work groupings in the Faith Workers' Branch but they are not a primary focus for its Executive Committee or the London-based Unite officers. These faith groupings are allocated a subordinate role within the dominant White culture of Unite. No wonder there are issues over identity which were picked up by New Labour with its citizenship courses and ceremonies to the Big Society concept of modern conservativism seeking to rework what it means to inhabit Britain.

Immigrant Host Relationships—A Brief History

It is not widely known that there have been Black people in what is now known as the UK for two thousand years, spanning from soldiers in the Roman empire, through Elizabethan times when we were sold here as slaves. After the First World War, Black soldiers, recently demobbed, decided to settle here. After the Second World War, Black people came here to answer the specific invitation of the British government of the day, with a campaign in the Caribbean led by Enoch Powell, a name that still resonates within the Black community. Carefully considering this history, we need to do theology and share the gospel from a context of identity politics that can get us past the immigrant host relationship model which is such a feature of many studies in this area. In terms of assimilation, Sheila Patterson, writing at a time of West Indian immigration to the UK, thought the ultimate social phase of assimilation was the complete adoption of the norms and patterns of the receiving society in her best-known text whose influence still lives on.[2] Adaptation denotes group and social change as opposed to adjustment which operates at the personal, individual level. Assimilation also requires the host society to be willing to accept the assimilating group. In her use of the term 'accommodation,' Patterson means the least degree of social change in all groups that will maintain peaceful co-existence; this is at the early phase of people movement. Thus, when she looked at Brixton she found minimal levels of adaptation and acceptance especially in the areas of economic life, housing, and many life issues including religious practice.

The accommodation she did look at entailed the unscrupulous methods of landlords charging high rents and racism rampant in the workplace. Even so, most newcomers found both work and somewhere to live, beginning the process of accommodation despite the great hostility openly shown by much of the receiving society. However, Patterson suggests that it was cultural differences more than racial discrimination that resulted in the conflict and tension between the communities. The receiving community of Brixton thought of itself as possessing the virtues typically associated with Englishness, propriety, quietness, respectability. The West Indian community was perceived almost as the polar opposite: noisy, gregarious, permitting common-law marriage. Yet Patterson believed there was a relatively benign attitude from the host society to these *Dark Strangers* as she called her book.[3] The immigrant-host paradigm also considered the pluralistic integrationist approach, where ethnic groups are organised separately retaining distinctive cultural patterns. Ivor Morrish thought that the process of integration can provide equal opportunities without eroding diversity.[4] These so-called sociological models were adopted both by the churches and by government, maintaining an immigrant-host dynamic in all areas of their debates.

• • •

2. Patterson, *Dark Strangers.*

3. Patterson, *Dark Strangers.*

4. Morrish, *Background of Immigrant Children.*

So, we find, according to the Swann Report, pluralism is defined as a process that encourages members of all ethnic groups,

> both minority and majority[,] to participate fully in shaping the society as a whole within a framework of commonly accepted values, practices and procedures, whilst also allowing and where necessary assisting the ethnic minority communities in maintaining their distinct ethnic identities within this common framework.[5]

This report advocated a multicultural education system. Britain was seen as a plural democracy which did not require the immediate social integration of ethnic minority communities even if this was a longer-term goal. The report drew attention to the poor educational performance of Bangladeshi pupils who would benefit from a greater acceptance of cultural diversity within the school environment. Pluralism actually only needs a minor degree of accommodation on the part of the host society as they tolerate the voyage to assimilation of the immigrants. Whatever model you use, British society is still highly discriminatory. True the modus operandi of racists has changed in response to new legislation but this does not preclude our use of theology to broker and enable better, warmer relationships that do not offend against the image of God in each one of us. The churches should be badgering government to look critically at social structures and provisions in order to facilitate genuine community cohesion.

Robert Runcie and the English Establishment

What follows is an account of Robert Runcie's leadership of the Church of England during the Thatcher era that built largely upon the edifice of Humphrey Carpenter's biography.[6] The interested public received this work as a reliable record of the Runcie Archiepiscopate. Carpenter's biography talks about Mrs Thatcher's involvement, as prime minister, in the appointment of bishops. The appointment of Graham Leonard as bishop of London is given some consideration although Runcie does not seem to remember very much about it.[7] He does remember that Graham Leonard was not the first name put forward and in response to the question as to whether Mrs Thatcher overrode the first choice, he conceded that it would be down to

---

5. "Swan Report," 5.
6. Carpenter, *Robert Runcie*.
7. Carpenter, *Robert Runcie*, 214.

her and that she was within her rights. Clearly, she had a political preference for someone whose sympathies were towards the right. Bernard Palmer describes Mrs Thatcher's role in the appointments of bishops as occasionally controversial but, placed alongside that of Victorian prime ministers, it would appear insignificant.[8] This is an observation which itself speaks loudly of the earlier relations between the state and the Church of England.

• • •

Carpenter's biography of Runcie also tells us that after the inner-city disturbance in the 1980s, he wrote to the home secretary, William Whitelaw, a fellow guards' officers and someone with whom he was on first-name terms. Runcie talks about Brixton as a place with intractable problems. Clearly, he sees it as his role as Archbishop of Canterbury to connect with the home secretary and offer some kind of help. Runcie expects to have a private and confidential reply and, indeed, the correspondence continues. This is interesting because at the same time Runcie says of himself that he is not a political animal and that he is better at responding to individuals than to widespread issues. Nevertheless, he was involved in such matters, affecting the life of the nation. He made a statement following the Scarman report and he went on to visit Toxteth.

Carpenter comments that by late 1981, following his Christmas sermon at Canterbury, Runcie was taking what was beginning to look like an anti-Thatcher line.[9] And Carpenter asks Runcie if he was able to communicate informally with the prime minister. Runcie's response was that she was not very good at inviting one round. Mrs Thatcher is reported to have claimed that Runcie was sounding off when all he had to do was warn her that he was feeling unhappy with government policies. Runcie tells us that Sir Geoffrey Howe would invite them round but not say anything that would suggest that the government thought he was wrong. Runcie continues to name drop the people he knew such as Jim Prior and Nigel Lawson and

> It was a bizarre state of affairs, that here was I, portrayed as hostile to this government, and on terms of friendship such as no archbishop has been this century. Norman St John Stevas was another one.[10]

8. Palmer, *High & Mitred*, 294.

9. Carpenter, *Robert Runcie*, 219.

10. Carpenter, *Robert Runcie*, 229.

There is ambivalence here and throughout the whole of this biography. Since Runcie really had all those personal connections with members of the government why didn't he use his influence to effect some significant change? The tone of what he says is very much along the lines that they were all in the guards together and what jolly chaps they were. There is nothing here resembling political analysis and debate. Perhaps it points to an additional linkage between church and the state; namely a peculiarly male/class network that operated upon shared experience and values.

The year 1981 was also when Robert Runcie conducted the wedding of the Prince and Princess of Wales. Runcie believes this to have been an arranged marriage but thinks they will grow into it. Runcie seems to have known about the relationship between Prince Charles and Camilla Parker-Bowles. He also knows that Prince Charles loves the language of the Prayer Book but is a little concerned that the prince may not love the Church of England very much. There are a number of personal comments about Diana. Runcie says that he is aware that if anything were said that is too abstract that she would not understand. He comments that all the women at court regarded her as an actress and a schemer.[11] So far as Runcie is concerned, this is all true.

Robert Runcie says that the person in the royal family that he really admires is the Queen:

> I don't fully understand her, but that's part of her secret. At moments of either high drama or pressure on me, like the papal visit or the coal miners' strike, she always went out of her way to encourage—it may have been indirectly, by an invitation to do something; it may have been by a chance word.[12]

At the level of wining and dining, clearly Runcie felt he had a good relationship with the royal family and particularly with the Queen. But how is that interpreted and shown publicly? One is left with the impression that Runcie regarded his time at Canterbury as a time of wining and dining with all sorts of influential people. There is nothing that comes out from this book to suggest that he found it a vocational challenge to be in prophetic opposition to the state. The emerging picture is of some sort of freeloader who has made good and who was enjoying the good times when he could

11. Carpenter, *Robert Runcie*, 222.
12. Carpenter, *Robert Runcie*, 224.

get them. Certainly, in Carpenter's biography, the sense of a man of integrity struggling with the challenge of radical Thatcherism is not clearly evident.

It is fascinating, and it says a great deal about Runcie, certainly a great deal about what Carpenter wanted to do with the book, that the chapter on what the job is contains so much more on the royals than all that was happening in the inner cities of Brixton, Toxteth, and so on. And that reflects how Runcie lived day to day. He lived as a kind of country gentleman or minor aristocrat in a social ambience that was strongly rooted in an English social system of privilege and personal networks.

You also get insights into how he actually handled his influence in the Anglican Communion. In the next chapter Runcie talks about how he maneuvered Tutu into episcopacy.[13] Terry Waite had said that this was an example of what other people might think of as intrigue but it was good diplomacy. It was quite clear that Runcie travelled the world a great deal and really did go out of his way to take note of the personal or more immediate circumstances of the various bishops that he met. According to Carpenter Runcie felt that there was a need for an ecumenical primate who would act as a focus person for the Christian community and that such a role could be filled by some sort of pope rather than the Archbishop of Canterbury.[14] So, on the one hand, he was going around at a personal level doing quite a good job of building a network of relationships but, on the other hand, in public, he was kind of stepping back from his role and almost denying it. This was to such an extent that in 1988, at the Lambeth conference of his arci-episcopate, the English bishops were amazed at the amount of influence and respect and affection that particularly the African bishops seemed to have for Runcie. It is interesting that it is the African bishops, because perhaps it is easier to 'help' Black people?

• • •

Runcie talks about relations with Rome. Again, it is in the same kind of style. There is no tackling of theological issues of either church politics or world politics. If Runcie and the pope had really got together and started to make some serious comments about oppression and world poverty, it would have been so much more effective. However, Runcie says that he cannot get worked up about things in that sort of way. It is as if it is not the

13. Carpenter, *Robert Runcie*, 229.
14. Carpenter, *Robert Runcie*, 234.

done thing to show enthusiasm. Maybe it is because Runcie was not born into the upper class that he has to behave as if he were.

We are informed that the Scarman Report was debated in the House of Lord's[15] Runcie was perceived as taking an anti-Thatcher stance when he said that the Church was determined not to abandon the inner city and retreat to suburbia. In February 1982, Runcie had said that it was time for a Black bishop. *The East Anglian Daily Times* reported that:

> The Archbishop of Canterbury Dr. Robert Runcie believes that it is time that the Church of England had a black bishop. Churches had to 'do their bit' in seeing that ethnic minorities were represented in positions of authority, Dr. Runcie said in an interview on a BBC TV programme for Asians yesterday.... He says the Church should achieve more in combating racial discrimination.... Instead of seeing the opportunities that come from having in our midst a rich diversity of people, we constantly see it as a problem. I don't. I see it as an opportunity.[16]

Carpenter also includes a report that appeared in *The Church Times*, 17th March 1982, which seems to be in contradiction to what had been said a month earlier, namely that

> Runcie had told a meeting of the National Society that he feared that this country's Christian tradition may be sacrificed on the altar of multi-culturalism.[17]

There would appear to be some kind of muddle here between what Carpenter thinks and what Runcie understands the situation to be. Perhaps for Runcie there is no contradiction between these statements.

• • •

In April 1982, Argentina invaded the Falkland Islands. There is a quotation in *The Times* from a speech which Runcie made supporting military intervention.[18] On the one hand, he is saying that sometimes you need to go to battle and whilst on the other hand you have got to pray for everybody. This is typical of the double think that Runcie does. Yes, it is just about possible that you can go into battle and pray for everybody but, if you are going into

15. Carpenter, *Robert Runcie*, 247.
16. Carpenter, *Robert Runcie*, 247.
17. Carpenter, *Robert Runcie*, 248.
18. Carpenter, *Robert Runcie*, 248.

battle and praying for everybody, why not just pray for every body and not go into battle? Even pray for peace? There does not seem to be any conviction that prayer works. The situation builds up until the service at the end of the conflict. Meanwhile, there is a papal visit to England. Two weeks after the Papal visit, Runcie issues a statement about the Falklands conflict which, according to Carpenter, pleased Mrs Thatcher. However, she was not pleased about the Service of Thanksgiving which was to follow. There was quite a lot said at the time about Mrs Thatcher's fury. Carpenter has a transcription of a telephone conversation with Lady Thatcher in which she said,

> I'm afraid I can't help you very much, which is why I didn't offer, because I don't know Lord Runcie anything like the extent that you think I do. And I don't want to be anything other than very nice about him. He's a very nice man. We always had very good relations, and I had of course met him when Dennis and I were dining with the Langs. The Runcies were sometimes there. I don't remember him at Oxford.[19]

Mrs Thatcher goes on to explain that she does not mention Runcie in her memories because in her words "there were no great church things during my time." This is fascinating because clearly there were, but that was her recollection. At this point Carpenter then goes on to ask her if she felt that the church was in any sense in opposition to her in view of what the press was saying. Mrs Thatcher's response is to say that she does not read the press particularly and that she relied on digests. Her response to a possible difference of opinion with Runcie over the Falklands Thanksgiving Service was as follows:

> Well, I don't really want to say anything against Lord Runcie. Some people said that you shouldn't celebrate victory. I thought when you were celebrating victory over aggression, you should do it— first you should beat the aggressor, which we did, then you should give thanks for the sacrifices that people had made in order that aggression should not prevail. And don't forget that Bob Runcie was a very brave person in the last war, and he was decorated.[20]

However, Mrs Thatcher does then go on to criticise the Thanksgiving Service, saying:

19. Carpenter, *Robert Runcie*, 259.
20. Carpenter, *Robert Runcie*, 260.

I felt that we didn't give, perhaps, sufficient recognition to all of those without whose sacrifice, and the skill with which the campaign was fought, the Falklands would not be free. And I must say that I do think it is right to make it clear that an aggressor shall never be appeased.[21]

Mrs Thatcher concludes what she has to say about this subject in the following tones:

I like Bob Runcie. He's a very, very good and honorable man, and I always enjoyed meeting him, and if ever we had genuine differences, they were differences between people who respected one another.[22]

Runcie says that he never wanted to be Archbishop of Canterbury and was very surprised to be asked. He seems to blame Richard Charters for persuading him to accept it. Part of Runcie's reluctance concerns a family crisis that was going on at the time. Following the publication of Margaret Duggan's *Runcie: the Making of an Archbishop* (1983), A. N. Wilson in an article in *The Spectator* referred to Runcie as a 'travel bore' who

seems to conceive his function as a sort of ecclesiastical foreign secretary, dashing about the world to attend boring conferences and spending most of his waking hours in airport lounges. Most politicians spend far too much of their time doing this sort of thing. But why should an Archbishop of Canterbury?[23]

In the same article, Wilson accuses Runcie of a "slithery absence of principle."[24]

Carpenter talks about the appointment of David Jenkins as Bishop of Durham, the striking of the York Minster by lighting and the striking of the coal miners. Runcie's first pronouncement on the latter was critical of the workforce. A sermon that Runcie gave at Derby Cathedral complained about violence on the picket lines. David Jenkins, the new Bishop of Durham, on the contrary, came out in support of the striking miners at his enthronement sermon. This seems to have been a trigger for Runcie to follow suit and change direction. Runcie was now telling the miners that it

21. Carpenter, *Robert Runcie*, 260.
22. Carpenter, *Robert Runcie*, 260.
23. Carpenter, *Robert Runcie*, 273.
24. Carpenter, *Robert Runcie*, 268.

was sometimes OK to stand in opposition to the government. He told *The Times*, 7 October 1984, that he could not support Thatcherite aims.

> If the human consequences of such aims mean unemployment on an unprecedented scale, poverty, bureaucracy, despair about the future of our communities, inequitable sharing of the sacrifice called for, then the objectives must be called in question.[25]

Runcie has been described as someone who liked nailing his colours to the fence. He has also been described as someone who liked to sit on his fence with his ear to the ground on both sides. It could be argued that this type of accommodation to all parties made Runcie, the man and the office, and consequently the church, look insincere, and unreliable. It is also quite clear that Runcie was very swayed by whomever he had spoken to last. He was very dependent upon advisers and sermon writers, script writers and all sorts, which we would expect, but there should be, within all that and out of his vocation as priest and bishop, some core of coherence—and it is not there. There is no central standard or tenant conveyed by Carpenter. Runcie described himself as being unable to get 'worked up' about lots of things. He could not get worked up about the ordination of women to the priesthood. He says that, unlike a lot of Evangelicals, he cannot think of Jesus as 'a pal.' Although we can understand his reluctance to such familiarity which might suggest an approach to the Christian faith which lacks reverence, nevertheless, it could be argued that if you have not got a sense of an infinite connection with a Saviour who is consistent in the way in which the world through him is both judged, condemned and rescued, then how can we live that forth? And it is the living forth that Runcie, through the pages of this biography, does not seem able to do. The TV programme *Spitting Image* had an ambiguous puppet for Runcie. It was ambiguous sexually, socially, theologically. According to Carpenter:

> [Runcie] was now becoming a regular target for mockery in the right-wing popular press. When in March 1985 he compared Britain's inner-city problems to the Ethiopian famine ("we do not have to look as far as Ethiopia to find the darkness of disease and death") the Daily Express headed its leader "Some silly words from Dr Runcie," and a Cummings cartoon showed Runcie in the pulpit of a crumbling ecclesiastical edifice, labelled "Church of England," saying: "We certainly don't have to look as far as Ethiopia to find the darkness of disaster—it's here on our doorstep!" The building

25. Wilson, "Doing the Lambeth Walk."

is already going up in flames, ignited by David Jenkins, who is clutching a large matchbox. The Star describes Runcie's comparison with Ethiopia as Clerical claptrap.[26]

When the *Faith in the City* report was published in 1985, *The Sunday Times* labelled it Marxist. Carpenter suggests that there was a smear campaign by the press to discredit Runcie. This took the form of *The Daily Star* and other national newspapers claiming that the archbishop and his wife lived separate lives. Carpenter says that this came from the highest quarters. He does not say that this campaign was Thatcher's revenge but it is certainly hinted at. Then comes the Terry Waite affair. Through the chapter 'St Terry' there is an old-style imperialist assumption of the British right to stick their nose in. Waite exemplifies that. Like Runcie, Waite was flying around the world as some type of troubleshooter. Runcie's approach here does seem to be: we are British and this is what we do.

The last chapter of the Carpenter biography is entitled 'A Classic Anglican'. *Runcie* is asked if he thinks there is any future for the sort of figure he has been as a 'Catholic Liberal' and he responded in the following manner:

> I think it's going to be quite difficult for the Archbishop to carry with him enough spiritual clout to be taken seriously at the center of the nation's life, because there is a distancing of church from state. I think there are fewer and fewer people who are involved in what makes the nation tick, either politically or culturally, who have their roots in the life of the church and the Christian faith.[27]

So how should we evaluate the Arci-episcopate of Robert Runcie that spanned the 1980s and was almost identically overlapped the premiership of Margaret Thatcher? The 1980s were difficult years for the British people. There was the Falklands war, the civil disturbances in Brixton, Toxteth and Handsworth and the miner's strike. The archbishop could have been the voice of righteousness in the nation. Even if all he did on behalf of the church was to pull people together who were in pain and hurting and ask where the right is, this did not have to be necessarily very political. But Runcie comes across, through the Carpenter biography, as neither overtly political nor spiritual. From this biography, you get an impression of a man who is vacillating; self-seeking, vain; and who liked going to posh parties. It could be argued that until *Faith in the City*, he served the purposes of the British

26. Carpenter, *Robert Runcie*, 275.
27. Carpenter, *Robert Runcie*, 371.

State very well. In a political era that was as self-serving and as self-seeking as the Thatcher years were, an archbishop without warmth or enthusiasm was just perfect. If Runcie had been on fire with the Christian gospel and with a genuine concern for the people, he could not have begun his relations with the public by telling the miners to behave themselves. Runcie as a figure of wincing, effeminate English masculinity, as seen in the *Spitting Image* puppet, expressed something about how people perceived him.

New Labour and Big Society—Same Horse, Different Jockey

New Labour had proclaimed that it welcomes immigration as being not merely beneficial to the economic life of the country but also as enrichment to the social and cultural milieu. This is rather difficult to maintain as more and more desperate people flee violence, largely created by the West, in areas such as Pakistan, Afghanistan, Zimbabwe and Somalia and social tensions flare in response to perceived favoritism to these groups as seen by local White populations. Furthermore, if culture is seen as including class, gender and religious membership then Britain is far more multicultural than New Labour actually wanted to acknowledge. Culture can be seen as a matrix of values and beliefs that enable sense to be made of experience; a shared collection of understandings of people living in the same context.

Whilst it is self-evident that in most societies there can be found a range of cultures based on class groups and other factors, in the UK, co-existence does not connote co-equality. The material means of production is controlled by the economically dominant groups who also control the mode of social conduct. With the collapse of the banking system in the late noughties, the moral vacuity of the consumer culture, the churches need to step in and promote other more real and beneficial values.

New Labour understood that it had to maintain an albeit uneasy alliance with those White people who feel that they are not as comfortable in their neighbourhoods as they once believed themselves to be. Solution? A single British identity with the multiculturalism of the past now seen as out-moded. The argument was very subtle: Britain has always had many cultures; there have always been a plurality of values and experiences; but life styles are now associated with racialised designations. New Labour, in reinventing the Labour Party in order to gain power and prominence, is not so far from the churches' desire to reinvent themselves in order to get bums on seats, as if the life of the church has ever been about quantity rather than quality. How much yeast do you actually need to make the dough rise? How much salt before the dish becomes uneatable? We were nurtured through New Labour in their inheritance of the conspicuous consumption ideals of the Thatcher era to think of more as better, bigger as greater. Where do we find that in the life of the Jesus of history or in the Christ of faith or in any conception of the divine mission?

So, what about the big society concept of modern conservatism? This is three decades on from Runcie and *Faith in the City*. What are the connections and implications for the Faith Workers' Branch with a form of government that is weak on welfare provision and strong on the virtues of a smaller state machine? Before we can answer this question, we need to set out clearly what this philosophy is actually about, coming as it does on the heels of New Labour and to the forefront of public opinion with the election of a conservative government in 2011. The big question at the time was: how do the churches and trade unions fit into the Big Society model? And will these institutions follow the move to localise and, in terms of the Anglican church, what might that look like? It is claimed that the British would rather do things for themselves than rely on a nanny state. The Big Society reckons that only by breaking away from the post-war dependency culture can people regain that confidence. The danger for the churches was that they could all too easily be seen as purpose-made to fit into the Big Society. We have two millennia of traditions of charitable and communitarian work, having tried to take seriously the second of the two dominical commandments. Moreover, we have the existing infrastructure with plant and personnel, both paid and volunteer, already in communities. We could be used to give credibility to the Big Society which appears to had adopted the Christian concept of neighborliness. We also see that we have to be interdependent, valuing all for who they are. This chimes with the Big Society mantra: *we are all in this together*. This explains the charm offensive being waged by the Big Society against, upon, the church.

At the time what seemed to been forgotten is that the churches have their own issues. When they are not fretting about internal issues of maintenance and fabric generally, then they tend to focus on a piece of outreach work either of practical charity such as support centres for refugees or in more obviously mission-centred activities. We can see how these can be seized as examples of the Big Society in action but it is crucial here to recall motivation. We need to be vigilant and examine our Christian consciences. Our prayer life must be guarded and this will lead us to question. Just because there is an element of truth in the Big Society argument, taken as a whole, it does not prevent this being built upon a lie. The Big Society seeks to dismantle sixty years of welfare, provision that the churches campaigned hard for to ensure parity of provision. To return to a position pre-welfare state would be a dangerous and a deeply anti-Christian act. This lie at the heart of the matter could explain why David Cameron and his regime had been obliged to relaunch the concept several times. This lie also caused the Big Society agenda to collapse under the weight of its inherent injustice much the same way that slavery did in the end.

Our faith has developed the concept of jubilee right through into the Acts of the Apostles with their aspiration to hold their goods and resources in common. Just because we cannot always reach a target does not mean we abandon it when it is intrinsically worthy and virtuous. This common life remains the Christian ideal. I do not hear any of that in the arguments of those who want small government; there is no economic reform being mooted. State monopoly capitalism will remain with the people perforce more distanced than ever, accountability further diminished. The Christian model and the Big Society are not commensurate at all, in fact, the opposite is the case.

In 2011, just before Pentecost Sunday, Rowan Williams, the then-Archbishop of Anglican published an article in *The New Statesman* to encourage a wider debate on the Big Society. Unfortunately, in choosing this medium, Rowan was largely addressing the chattering classes in a typically ivory tower fashion. However, he did focus on the widespread view that the Big Society is an opportunistic, not to say cynical, way of cutting public services. He refers to the Big Society as a "painfully stale" term. He sought to define democracy and referred to "bafflement and indignation" displayed by the voters who did not give the government a mandate at the last general election. He implies through this that the Big Society is undemocratic although he does not go quite that far overtly.

It is regrettable that it took the archbishop a whole year in the life of the Cameron government before he could actually condemn the re-use of the language of the deserving and the undeserving poor. He draws attention to the very real public fear concerning the Big Society: fears about poor literacy, child poverty, unfair educational provision, etc. He refers to popular "anxiety and anger" with regard to the lack of transparency and the headlong rush to change and change again. He looks at some of the changes in education but he does not examine health. There is, he claims, genuine confusion over the practicalities of the Big Society and over quality assurance issues if there are few national benchmarks. Youth services should be a priority but they are being cut left, right, and centre. He queries if there are some matters too important to be left to local oversight and management. He uses Pauline references to discuss communality. The church should be at the forefront of public debate and interrogation of the politics of the day yet the view still persists that the gospel is somehow apolitical; it is almost unseemly for clergy to do mission through tackling politics. We have left our people in darkness, ignorant of their past and uncertain as to the future.

Jesse Norman, a fan of Big Society saw this approach as a set of ideas linked around the mechanisms of government and based upon a citizenship that actively seeks self-reliance.[28] This notion requires deregulation and localisation, resources moved from the control of the centre out to the localities. This, it is hoped, will engender a more connected society as people come together to determine how they will share out those resources. So, at the heart of the Big Society agenda is the desire to change the way we think about and behave towards the relationship between the state and individuals.[29] Transferring power from the centre in this way presupposes that there are enough skilled local groups who can rise to this task, groups such as co-ops, charities, etc. Under the banner of community empowerment, all government departments were charged to work in this way, especially the Department of Work and Pensions, in order to get people off benefits and into gainful employment. So, was the government of the day really doing this for the common good? What is the true agenda? What if we spiral into even greater inequalities as local skills vary so greatly? Leafy Surrey is going to be able to make very different use of resources as opposed to many people where I used to live in inner-city Birmingham.

Norman is prepared to address the fact that the Big Society has its critics whom he puts into five categories. He starts by denying that the very notion of the Big Society enshrines a vagueness of definition although he does allow some ambiguity around the edges. Predictably, Norman blames New Labour for the current economic woes whereas the merits of the Big Society are that it is not a similar top-down strategy hence the need for some inbuilt

28. Norman, *The Big Society*, 195.

29. Norman, *The Big Society*, 199.

flexibility.[30] A second criticism is met with a robust denial that the Big Society is good for government because it works in the national interest.[31]

Norman also denies a third criticism that the Big Society depends on the Third Sector as public services disappear.[32] Rejecting a fourth area of criticism, he says that this is not a return to Thatcherism, completely rejecting the claim that the Big Society is merely a cover, an ideological smokescreen, for swingeing cuts; rather Norman seeks to trace the origins of the Big Society to the eighteenth century.[33] This means that the Big Society has nothing at all to do with the cuts. And anyway, he alleges, some cuts are obligatory to offset the excesses of the previous Labour regime whose topheavy and over-centralised structures have to be dismantled. Regrettably some good causes will suffer in the national interest[34]—presumably our stiff upper lips will see us through!

• • •

A similar theme is expressed by Tory management gurus, Matthew Bishop and Michael Green, who explained at the time that the arts and higher education will have to get their funding from corporate interest and private charities.[35] It comes as no surprise that these two also strongly refute that the Big Society is Thatcherism with a new name.[36] I agree that New Labour did encourage responsible entrepreneurism and competition in public service provision but this was explained as a means of adding value to people's lives and to their commitment to community.[37] Are we seriously to believe that the big investors actually wanted to invest in the wellbeing of the disadvantaged and marginalised from sheer philanthropy?[38] Even more difficult to believe is that the Big Society agenda would result in real oversight of business leaders, giving the consumer the control over capitalist production.[39] Bishop and Green see a popular capitalism benefi-

30. Norman, *Big Society*, 200.

31. Norman, *Big Society*, 200.

32. Norman, *Big Society*, 200–201.

33. Norman, *Big Society*, 201–2.

34. Norman, *Big Society*, 202.

35. Bishop and Green, *Road from Ruin*, 309.

36. Bishop and Green, *Road from Ruin*, 308.

37. Bishop and Green, *Road from Ruin*, 308.

38. Bishop and Green, *Road from Ruin*, 309.

39. Bishop and Green, *Road from Ruin*, 310.

cently making money and providing for all. They call this *Gross National Happiness*—gross perhaps best glossed in its vernacular sense![40]

Norman's last category of criticism came from the academic world via *The Spirit Level* by Richard Wilkinson and Kate Pickett.[41] These writers saw improved social outcomes as being crucial. They do not have a problem with higher taxation and redistribution of incomes to effect social wellbeing.[42] This bothers Norman but he goes on to claim that *The Spirit Level* can fit into the Big Society model.[43] But is this a fair reading of the work? *The Spirit Level* is packed full of data and graphs that are not as interesting or as surprising as their authors appear to claim. Most of the ideas and the methods of data collection can be found in another publication by Wilkinson, namely *The Impact of Inequality*.[44] However in the *Spirit Level* the statistics are balanced out and made more accessible by a series of clever cartoons one of which has an explicit political message: if rich people are going to take a disproportionate amount of the financial wealth for themselves, including tax cuts, leaving very little for the rest of us, then they cannot, at the same time, expect a clean and healthy environment.[45]

Wilkinson and Picket note the disparity between the material achievements of prosperous countries and the social failure of those societies and see this as an indicator of the effect of inequality. In Britain, the broken society of 2008 soon became the broken economy of the same period.[46] It is interesting that, after the civil disturbances of August 2011, there was great resistance by many politicians and church leaders to relate social unrest to economic failure or to public spending cuts. For Wilkinson and Picket, inequality was a characteristic of social structure in any given society which requires some alteration.[47] The focus of their work is to show how these disparities of wealth are detrimental to the wellbeing of the majority of people through epidemiological analysis of economic inequality. Psychology and individual perception have a part to play in the feel-good factor of modern life. This is not a matter of individual psychology although the worst effects

40. Bishop and Green, *Road from Ruin*, 311.

41. Wilkinson and Pickett, *Spirit Level*.

42. Wilkinson and Pickett, *Spirit Level*, 271.

43. Norman, *Big Society*, 203.

44. Wilkinson, *Impact of Inequality*.

45. Wilkinson and Pickett, *Spirit Level*, 2.

46. Wilkinson and Pickett, *Spirit Level*, 4–5.

47. Wilkinson and Pickett, *Spirit Level*, 13.

are felt by the individual who is on the receiving end of social and fiscal policy decisions.[48] Increased levels of mental illness and behavioral problems among young people can all be linked to the level of inequality, an interestingly poignant point post-August 2011 with the extreme civil unrest that swept parts of the country. Furthermore, they concluded that social status can be related to inequality with the latter becoming more important in those societies that have the greatest differentials in material wealth. In this context, social mobility is seen as the mechanism that gives weight to rewards for actual ability[49] which, from my point of view, is important in making sense of institutions like White majority historical churches that allocate responsibilities on the basis of who you know rather than what you know. For Wilkinson and Picket, inequality is associated with the twin concepts of *status competition* and *status anxiety*.[50] Pertinent to the civil disturbances of August 2011, inequalities can also link to the amount of violence in UK society which will weaken cohesion.[51] Wilkinson and Picket present to their readers a time line as to the development of freedom and of human progress. For them, things start off with low levels of equality under slavery but improved with universal suffrage, employment rights and the development of a welfare state.[52] For these writers, the preconditions for a Big Society are already there in state welfare provision which has majority support. The argument is that if we narrow the gap between income groups, people would be able to empathise with each other and promote a real sense of community. The knock-on effect would be a reduction in obesity, mental illness, and under-age pregnancies.[53] Clearly if there was a significant level of equality in the UK, then David Cameron's idea that *we are all in it together* would not be so absurd.

To claim that more equal societies are healthier than less equal societies is to engage in a level of relativism that begs as many questions as it answers. If inequality is relative then so is poverty, yet most of us would argue that there are certain basic requirements to sustain what could be understood as human existence. Thus, the universality of the propositions contained in *The Spirit Level* are questionable. Would we want to aspire to

48. Wilkinson and Pickett, *Spirit Level*, 32–33.
49. Wilkinson and Pickett, *Spirit Level*, 43.
50. Wilkinson and Pickett, *Spirit Level*, 44.
51. Wilkinson and Pickett, *Spirit Level*, 45.
52. Wilkinson and Pickett, *Spirit Level*, 268.
53. Wilkinson and Pickett, *Spirit Level*, 268–69.

a situation of a very poor but equal society where everyone pulls together in extreme poverty? If the UK and the West were in such a case, would we have to worry about depression and anxiety or any of the other social problems associated with consumerism? Clearly welfare provision, a major plank of equality, would no longer be there.

• • •

The Spirit Level definitely requires a clear conclusion. The obvious outcome of this work is to call for a socialist economic system but Wilkinson and Picket stop short at this, apparently preferring to wait for other people to do their political work for them. These writers do challenge the legitimacy of bankers' bonuses, believing them to be part of a culture which compromises the common good and wellbeing of the majority of the world's population. They advocate a more equal society which would bring about environmental sustainability and at the same time be good for the economy. But there lies the question: what economic system do they want? The things they don't like about capitalism strike me as integral to the state monopoly stage of that system. Wilkinson and Picket do talk about the non-profit making sector and employee-ownership schemes but fail to relate this back in any serious way to the excess of the market system that they want to disown.[54] Interesting? Yes. Definitive? No.

The English Identity Crisis

A further layer of complexity is how the terms 'British' and 'English' are used. What about the historical colonialisation of the Celts by the descendants of the Germanic invaders of early history in these islands, not to mention the rationality expressed in group identification dividing North and South, Yorkshire from Lancashire, Cornish from the rest? Once again, the rest have to define themselves as opposed to the Home Counties English who become typified, to themselves, as calm and lordly, serenely above the emotional and erratic temperament of the Celtic others. These others perceive the English as reserved, cold and patronizing. All this is obviously painted in very broad brushstrokes but sociology's job is precisely to identify and decode these into a more humane and accessible discourse. From a theological perspective what is clear is that these islands have fracture at the

54. Wilkinson and Pickett, *Spirit Level*, 252–63.

centre of perceived self-identity which is precisely where the unifying and blessing-filled mantle of Christ can usher in healing and harmony.

The entire debate about citizenship however continues to be seen not as who the inhabitants of these islands truly are but how they are holding up against the hordes of foreign others flocking to our shores or commando crawling through the Channel tunnel. We routinely welcome survivors of pilgrimages of agony and courage by clapping them in prison, even their children. During the days of overt Empire, the plucky sons of these tiny islands went out into a world to bring order into chaos, justice into irrationality. These activities, especially in the post reformation context, isolated the British until they had to tell themselves their own story very loudly and at all times and in all places. As the missionaries took the Bible and exchanged it for territory it became more important than ever that Britishness connoted righteousness despite the obvious contrariety of the actual, external reality of the day. This reactive defensiveness continues to be visible today. Within this, the Anglican Church had perforce become a repository of exclusivity and oppression.

The nostalgic preoccupation with the past continues to tie England and the English people not only to an ambiguous relationship to other nationality groups within the UK but also and more importantly to a notion of civil society. Phillip Blond, another fan of the Big Society concept, claimed that all political parties that have ever been in government should take responsibility for the erosion of British civil life.[55] He says that this has been squeezed by the two forces of free capital markets and the state itself. Blond asserts that once autonomous groups, including churches, trade unions and co-operatives, are all victims to this process and have lost their independence. He identifies one type of exception to this as single-issue campaign groups whose life span tends to be limited anyway by virtue of the nature of such groups.[56] Blond therefore accuses both left and right of killing off civil society. They have done this through local government who wanted to expand their operations by abolishing smaller units of democracy claiming that they were not cost effective.[57] Blond sees Thatcher as strengthening the state because she wanted to increase the power of the market.[58] New Labour followed a similar path, surrendering the interests of

55. Blond, *Red Tory*.
56. Blond, *Red Tory*, 3.
57. Blond, *Red Tory*, 4.
58. Blond, *Red Tory*, 4.

ordinary individuals to the demands of markets and the big banks.[59] This focus over the last three decades has damaged not just civil society but also torn apart the extended family structure and now threatens, Blond claims, the nuclear family.[60] The British way of life, whatever that might be, has disappeared in reality. Because we know that we have no real say in either local or national government, we have turned our backs on other organisations such as the churches.[61]

Once again, the retrospective rosy spectacles are in use when it comes to describing what it means to be British. We need Betjeman more than ever! Blond alleges that the rot set in with the enclosure of land, that before then, there was a prosperous peasantry up to Tudor times that gradually disappeared at the time of the Civil War so that the Industrial Revolution saw these relatively wealthy peasants ejected from their lands to be condemned to labour in factories.[62] This explains why the modern industrial proletariat has a history of resentment towards central government.[63] Blond argues that, under New Labour with its fixation on league tables and benchmarks and targets as tools of state control, government is seen as the opposition to civil liberties and directly responsible for the massive national debt.[64] The working class had been turned into a passive recipient of consumer capitalism.[65]

The oligarchy of New Labour is both the producer and the product of what is seen as an unholy relationship between state and the capitalist market, combining public authoritarianism with private liberalism.[66] In that light, the Big Society is presented as a transformative process using shared assets for welfare provision based on civil mutualism.[67] This agenda would therefore engage the enthusiasm and commitment of the frontline workforce as it co-operatively draws upon the notions of a free market

59. Blond, *Red Tory*, 4–5.

60. Blond, *Red Tory*, 7.

61. Blond, *Red Tory*, 7.

62. Blond, *Red Tory*, 11.

63. Blond, *Red Tory*, 14–15.

64. Blond, *Red Tory*, 21.

65. Blond, *Red Tory*, 22.

66. Blond, *Red Tory*, 27.

67. Blond, *Red Tory*, 32.

capitalism.[68] The Big Society thus restructures communal and individual relationships through the removal of central control of welfare provision.[69]

The old Tory siren song that an Englishman's home is his castle has been updated, given a makeover. But who actually wants to live in a castle anyway—draughts, no heating, antiquated plumbing, not to mention the issue of servants, let alone the trouble of moat upkeep? This blithe assumption of autonomy leads to a category of spoilers, people who cannot, for whatever reason, even aspire to independence. These people deserve punishment for breaking the rules. No surprises there then that those hapless and helpless persons on long-term benefits fit seamlessly into this cruel category of undesirables, hence, presumably, the insistence of government that the August 2011 riots were acts of pure criminality and nothing else.

Patrick Wright's seminal work *On Living in a Old Country* and his concept of 'Deep England' has some very clear application for the Big Society agenda.[70] It sees the past not so much as a replacement for the present but as an active participant in its reconstruction. For Wright 'Deep England' represents a mythicised heritage whose construction arises out of Britain's lost position on the world stage and typified by its marginalised status in Europe and the wider world. Deep Englishness is an interpretative framework that allows us to make sense of a *national past* that only existed in the selective memory of a privileged few.[71] This imaginary Britain, and the invitation to participate in its reproduction, is a compensation for a past that the majority of Britons never had. The nostalgia of 'Deep England' provides security in an insecure environment. It taps into a psychological desire for a better past that can be re-valued, reconstructed and elevated to that of a national heritage. Thus the national identity is a modern construction which can be defined in relation to the prevailing political climate.[72]

According to Wright the increasing public emphasis placed upon national identity during the Thatcher years is symptomatic of the political crisis that also characterises that era. The Thatcher regime required cultural meaning to legitimate itself.

> In this situation tradition appears as artifice, articulated not in particular or essential connection to people's experience, but at

68. Blond, *Red Tory*, 239.
69. Blond, *Red Tory*, 290–91.
70. Wright, *On Living in an Old Country*.
71. Wright, *On Living in an Old Country*, 77–83.
72. Wright, *On Living in an Old Country*, 127.

the generalized and diffuse level of an overriding "national" identity. The "nation" of this concern therefore has no easy relation to the existence and historical development of the nation-state; it is instead a structuring of consciousness, a publicly instituted sense of identity which finds its support in a variety of experiences, and which is capable of colonizing and making sense of others. Among its most fundamental elements is a historically produced sense of the past which acts as ground for a proliferation of other definitions of what is normal, appropriate or possible.[73]

Thus the 'national past' as expressed in history, national heritage and tradition becomes a national present in the social reality of the public domain. This politically constructed past is not to be confused with the concept of history but rather stands in opposition to a critical historical consciousness. For Wright the *national past* is a public understanding of the past events in the life of the nation that is too explicit to be thought of as just tradition.[74] The *national past* is reproduced through state institutions as a public present.[75] Reproductions include commemorations of national events, landscapes and old buildings. This national understanding of the past is a defense of a national heritage which is publicly understood to be under threat, thus making the characteristic in question definitional and internal to its own problematic. For Wright the 'national past' is perpetuated through public agencies of social control which have the effect of creating out-groups who are, by definition, perceived as alien to the national interest.[76]

Wright identifies four different ways of understanding the past in its relationship to the present. He uses the term 'past-present alignments' to show how representations of the past become legitimisation for contemporary social and political phenomenon.[77] These alignments include the 'complacent bourgeois alignment' that is concerned with maintaining the status quo by rejoicing in the present as the successful realisation of an historical process that is now completed. Thus, the present is good, worth waiting for, and, above all, worth protecting.[78] The second alignment, the 'anxious aristocrat alignment', comes into play when the first alignment

73. Wright, *On Living in an Old Country*, 128.
74. Wright, *On Living in an Old Country*, 129.
75. Wright, *On Living in an Old Country*, 131.
76. Wright, *On Living in an Old Country*, 132.
77. Wright, *On Living in an Old Country*, 133.
78. Wright, *On Living in an Old Country*, 134.

fails as a legitimizing tool and confidence in the prevailing order is lost. Now people have to recognise that the well-ordered and civilised society has gone before something of its former greatness can be restored. The only way to halt this national betrayal plunging us into barbarism is to adopt a patriotism which calls upon us to guard our heritage before it is really too late.[79]The 'complacent bourgeois alignment' and the 'anxious aristocrat alignment' come out of very different political interests nevertheless they work well together in the preservation of the national heritage. Old buildings are something tangible and worth keeping and, at the same time, understood by the public interest as under threat from the prevailing moral decline. The 'anti-traditional technicist alignment' perceives history as a negative collection of out-of-date relics. Trade unions, with their concepts of solidarity, closed shop, and picket line fall into this category. Mrs Thatcher expressed this selective view of the past when she accused Arthur Scargill, the miners' leader, of wanting to turn Britain into a museum society.[80] Wright's fourth alignment is that of the 'marching proletariat alignment.' Here we are concerned with how the Labour Movement has perceived the past as a class struggle that leads eventually to socialism via the dictatorship of the proletariat. This alignment is now in crisis as there are no concrete expressions of socialism left in the present upon which inspiration can be drawn. It can only really exist as an idea that stands in critical challenge to the present.[81]

England stands alone, literally in its island status, aside from mainstream Europe Protestantism. So, Whiteness, Englishness and religion form a potent mix where the isolation of the English is proudly held. Remember the old joke: There is a fog in the Channel and the Continent is cut off. The development of empire deepened this sense of otherness from the rest of Europe. It is no coincidence that at the height of colonial expansion, this country was sending out waves of missionaries. There was no serious challenge to imperial expansion by any neighbour culture until the Second World War. This estrangement from the rest of Europe goes some way to explain the reactive nature of English identity as well as the way in which the national church had already become a repository of oppression. Standing against European Catholicism gave the English church plenty of opportunity to develop sophisticated modes of exclusion, some very subtle indeed.

79. Wright, *On Living in an Old Country*, 134.
80. Wright, *On Living in an Old Country*, 136–37.
81. Wright, *On Living in an Old Country*, 139.

It was this need to achieve identity in solitude that united the otherwise fractured racial and cultural identities of the many groups in these islands. So, in the late forties and early fifties as the Caribbean people flowed at the call of the motherland to rebuilt the battered home of the scattered children of empire, they were not greeted with the gratitude that they expected and hoped for. And the Church of England was no exception.

Patrick Wright expounds the notion of *Deep England* as something that never actually existed but was mutually developed out of a lament for the glories of the past and a desire for certainty in a changing world. For this reason, it is not surprising that the Big Society would want to enlist the services of the church, and that of the Church of England in particular, as a sign post to a Deep Anglicanism bound in reverie to its past, still perpetuating the very structures of Empire in its worldwide network. As the established church, the Church of England has a uniquely influential role in the life of the nation, for example, only its bishops, thus far, have crowned the heads of state. The Royal Family, itself a marker of Englishness despite a very mixed heritage, sums up all that conventional piety betokens. There are still rules about who in the Royal Family may or may not marry a Roman Catholic. The Duchess of Cambridge felt obliged to be confirmed prior to her marriage conducted under the auspices of the Church of England in a ceremony that used outdated liturgies to emphasise that not all has changed for the worst. Westminster Abbey is usually the place where these great state occasions are carried out. Here lie the heroes of Englishness, the fallen in battle, the artists. Even though the role of the church in everyday life has diminished, it is still therefore reasonable to present the church as a pivotal signifier of Englishness.

So, how do we conclusion this chapter? We have tried to make some sense of a relationship between the direction of travel for the Faith Workers' Branch of Unite the Union and the single British identity inherited from New Labour. Faith Worker politics would fit better into that historical context than into any contemporary realisation. Margaret Thatcher accused the unions of her day of living in the past and I find myself from a very different direction saying the same thing of unions who claim to promote the wellbeing of those who work for a faith organisation. *There is a fog in the channel* is very much the approach of the cabal who run the Faith Workers' Branch. In this chapter I also considered issues of ethnicity and identity politics within the historical context of the Big Society. To put it bluntly, I believe that the politicians and their pet theorists simply wanted to defend their continued exploitation of the British public for the private profit of the few. They cloak their purposes in seeming philanthropy which is all too easily exposed. Talk to people on the bus and they will soon tell you. Furthermore, during this historical period, the scandal of phone hacking continued to flare and the seat of government was routinely shaken thereby as we see played out in public the very problem of the Big Society with its intrinsic lack of accountability. The vulnerable and needy in our society should not have to turn to enlightened self-interest to be treated with the dignity and the assistance that they deserve by virtue of their very existence. The Christian concept of humanity as *in imago dei* is crucial. We are each precious, not just some of us. It seems to me that a true witness to the kingdom is the realisation of the imperative for universal care. That, I hear you say, sounds like socialism and so it does for that is the root of socialism after all. I call upon the church to do more than accept this but to embrace it, ardently advocate it. Jesus overturned the tables of the money changers. Go and do likewise.

Chapter Three

Decision-Making, Workplace Groupings and a Review

IN THIS CHAPTER I will consider a number of decisions that were made by the acting chair on behalf of the Faith Workers' Branch and later reported to the Branch meeting and Executive Committee. These actions involved detailed consultations with Unite officials to which I was excluded and my position as Branch Secretary was seriously undermined. Conflict within the branch was centred around the formation of work place groupings of Muslim and Hindu members. These new structures were eventually approved but this was followed by a Unite review of the way the branch functioned.

We start with the chair's action. At the branch meeting in September 2019 the acting chair gave a lengthy report about what she had been doing since taking office. It was explained in some detail that there are times when as chair, she had the opportunity to act on behalf of the whole Faith Workers' Branch. We were informed that because our national branch was hosted by the London & Eastern Region of Unite, it was appropriate for them to make certain recommendations for changes in the way our branch operates, and that they proposed that discussions be held with our National and Regional Officers to move this forward. It was anticipated that such a review may take time but the wheels could be put in motion soon. Members asked if there's going to be a review, what would be the scope of that review? Would it be a greater review and allow members to have influence over how they want to see their Branch working? The acting chair explained that the review that was being recommended would be mainly internal focusing on how we operate as a multifaith organisation, and how we support people of all faiths, within our Branch. So, this was the alleged priority. I was branch secretary but knew nothing about this until this meeting of members. The acting chair continued her report. Since September, as part of this new role in following up helpline issues and recognising that over 53 percent of members are Church of England clergy, she had a meeting with the Church of England Pensions Board Welfare Officer to clarify the position regarding clergy who need to take early retirement due to stress or other illness. Members were informed that they had a direct line of contact should they face this situation.

As a follow-up on the twenty-fifth anniversary celebration, the acting chair along with the treasurer were invited to a meeting with the Deputy General Secretary of Unite, and a Unite National Officer to look at how the branch might move forward for the next twenty-five years. Readers will recall from a previous chapter that this was a meeting to which I had been excluded. This would be followed by other meetings to consider prioritizing and resourcing. I did not receive an invite to these meetings. It was acknowledged that priority had been given to the needs of Anglian clergy but that where we had made change happen in the Church of England there has been a "roll through" to the Methodists. In the most patronizing of tones, it was explained that we will be looking at how we can devote time to the other faith groups so that they are not lagging behind. The acting chair concluded her long report by saying that being part of Unite has real advantages for our scattered members, but especially the free specialist training our reps receive and the support of our dedicated Helpline. In return, we have a responsibility to act and work within the framework of Unite, while being ready to recommend change where that will benefit the majority of our members, and not disadvantage others.

From the floor, members asked, isn't the Branch Meeting the chance for members to give their opinion about what we should be doing? The response from the chair was that we are hoping we would deal with that sort of thing in an agenda item before the date of next meeting. As secretary I informed the meeting that there are some issues that have come to me from members. The acting chair asked if these might come up in the secretary's report? I explained that these were issues which related to member comments and that they had given up their time to come here, and we should listen to them. They were unlikely to be interested in long reports from branch officers.

So, what about recognition of new workplace groupings? This was a subject of interest for members who had attended meetings in support of these developments. On 28th January, 2020 at the Bristol Regional Office, Tony Benn House, the Faith Workers' Branch had an agenda item on faith work groupings. It was about the recognition of the 'Association of Hindu Faith Workers' and 'Muslim Faith Workers', as workplace groupings. The Branch was allowed to organise separate sub-groups to represent members in relation to a specific denomination, faith group or other working context, which shall be recognised as Unite Workplace Groupings. According to the standing orders such sub-groups shall have their own constitution and standing orders, which shall not be inconsistent with those of the Branch or Unite. The groupings currently recognised were Church of England Clergy Advocates (CECA), Association of Methodist Faith Workers (AMFW) and Unitarian and Free Christian Association (UCFA).

The acting chair explained that the rationale for forming these sub-groups within the Faith Workers' Branch had been that all potential members must be authorised by a common body whether as office holders or as employees and subject to the same disciplinary process. There must be a sufficient potential pool of eligible people with a good percentage already in the Branch to warrant existing Faith Workers' Branch members setting up a committee with a minimum of three officers for the purpose of organizing together to improve their conditions of service. Once these provisions are met a draft constitution should be drawn up, approved by the Faith Workers' Branch Exec and passed to the Community Youth and Not for Profit Sector legal services for recognition. We were then told that the new workplace group may have an informal shadow committee but will only be established by elections and vote at the next triennial General Meeting of the Faith Workers' Branch.

Again, in patronizing tones, we were told that the union would love to see enough Muslims and Hindus within the branch for such subgroups to be set up but that unfortunately we didn't have the numbers for this to proceed at this time. The acting chair had been advised that though we can have a brief discussion now, no votes can be taken today but there would be time before the next triennial in Spring 2021 for these workplace groupings to be approved. From the chair we were informed that we have due processes that should be followed within Unite and they have not been followed. Muhammad Al-Hussaini pointed out that the suggestion that a critical number of members from a particular tradition need to be present for a workplace grouping to be set up is contrary to the rule book. There was nothing in the rule book to stop this from happening at this meeting. The rule book is the constitution of the Union and the rule book is the point at which Muhammad Al-Hussaini and others had organised workplace groupings.

From the chair we were told that at this present time, we were advised that we should not take on any new workplace groupings, and that she would be grateful if we would accept that as a ruling from the chair. At this point another member of the Executive Committee intervened and said she was deeply concerned about the fact that we have asked people to come to the Branch Meeting and it has got so complex, or so heated. She said she was rather concerned that the chair didn't bring this up when the national officer was present through Skype, at the beginning of the meeting. She thought that would have been a better way of chairing this meeting. Could she respectfully ask, if there are going to be contentious areas, we do them at the right time when the right officers are present? And if it becomes highly contentious between two people, then she would say perhaps we need someone else to take the chair, just to calm things down.

• • •

The acting chair responded by saying that she was under instruction that no vote should be taken at this meeting in respect of this request. And as such she was not going to allow a vote to be taken at this meeting. She went on to say that she apologised for the fact that the member was not notified beforehand but she only received the information today so was unable to give any advance warning. The branch treasurer made a point of order that in light of the advice that the chair had received we move to next business which was seconded by the helpline co-ordinator. Other members of the branch said they would like to contribute to this debate. They thought it's only fair that people be heard when they feel aggrieved, and we should be discussing this and pointed out that the Executive Committee was not fully representative of the communities concerned. It was put to a vote with seven in favour and eight against the motion to proceed to next business. The motion was lost and the debate continued.

Muhammad Al-Hussaini commented and reinforced the position that the issues that have been raised are to do with the rule book, the standing orders and the timely submission of documents for this application for workplace groupings. As Branch Secretary at the time, I can confirm that all of these were complied with and I recorded this in the minutes.[1] Muhammad Al-Hussaini went on to say that in relation to the Equality Act 2010 and the fact that this Branch is subject to the purview of the Equality Act no member shall be discriminated against by reason of their membership or religion or other personal characteristic within the Faith Workers' Branch and that just doesn't pertain to the existence of committees it also pertains to the allocation of resources and money to services in the interests of the Hindu community, Sikh community and so forth. Muhammad Al-Hussaini contested the numbers upon which the acting chair relied as being speculative.

On 15th May 2020, the Unite Legal Department wrote a letter to the Unite Faith Workers' Branch Executive Committee in which they stated, "We have seen and considered the applications from members of the Faith Workers' Branch to create Muslim and Hindu workplace groupings and consider them to be eligible for approval by the Branch as distinct subgroupings in line with the current practice of the Branch". How big of them. The letter goes on to say, "We would therefore recommend that at the next available opportunity the Branch Executive Committee approve the two new sub groups with a review of activity and membership numbers to take place at the next AGM". However, when this came to committee the resolution was changed to that of only recognition of the constitutions of Muslim faith workers and the Association of Hindu faith workers. So, the Unite Faith Workers' Branch Executive Committee had not voted to adopt the governance documents of both ethnic and religious minority Workplace Groupings but just its recognition in principle. It would seem they were going to drag their feet every step of the way. On 18th September 2020 the results of a vote were confirmed for full recognition and implementation of

1. "We are complying with the Rule Book and we are complying with the Standing Orders. If you have custom, if you have precedent that we happen to do that on a triennial basis, those customs can be overridden for different purposes and we do not have to wait for the triennial meeting for a workplace grouping to be recognised because it doesn't say that it has to happen either in the Rule Book or in the Standing Orders. I submitted the constitution in very good time. If there has been a failure to submit it to committees that you're saying it should have been submitted to, that is your fault, Ruth, and that is your fault as an office holder, so I would insist that you apologise for failing to submit the documents that have been provided to you in good time to relevant committees. As far as compliance with the Rule Book of Unite the Union is concerned and the Standing Orders of the Faith Workers' Branch is concerned all of those matters have been complied with. If you're making up thresholds for things to be set up then that is wrong." (Faith Workers' Branch minutes 28th January 2020 at Bristol Regional Office, Tony Benn House, Victoria Street, Bristol, BS1 6AY).

these workplace groupings within the Unite Faith Workers' Branch. So, at last the Unite Faith Workers' Branch Executive Committee voted via email with immediate effect to confirm the full (and not partial or embryonic) recognition of Muslim and Hindu faith workers as a recognised Workplace Grouping of the Unite Faith Workers' Branch. It was agreed to mandate Muhammad to liaise with me and others to develop a joint project and budget to address issues of representation of ethnic and religious minorities within the Unite Faith Workers' Branch. So, it was recommended that Muslim faith workers adopt a common position in solidarity with me as Branch Secretary and the Chair of the Association of Hindu faith workers.

The Muslim workplace grouping would address institutional racism and sectarianism within the Unite Faith Workers' Branch, Unite the Union and elsewhere. The disproportionate impact of COVID-19 upon ethnic and religious minorities and their places of worship was also to form part of this initiative. They would be addressing issues of institutional abuse, bullying and victimisation within churches and other faith-based organisations. In particular, given their very considerable collective experience of these matters, it was agreed that they would collaborate with clergy, abuse solicitors, survivors and other campaigners. It was unanimously agreed that a budget for these projects, meetings and training for Workplace Grouping Members be developed jointly with their sister Workplace Grouping, the Association of Hindu faith workers, working with our Christian and other colleagues of good faith, in order to build up structures for campaigning in the public domain and collective bargaining with employing faith-based organisations. The aims of the Hindu workplace grouping are to provide the means of independent representation and support for member clergy and faith workers who find a need for advice or representation in the conduct of their relationship with employing and authority structures or with congregations or others among whom they work.

So, what are the matters of concern here? The allegation made by Muhammad Al-Hussaini and myself that the Unite Faith Workers' Branch is institutionally racist and institutionally sectarian is not made lightly, but rather from our prior academic scholarship in this area and our close observation and discussion with legal counsel of documents, statements and behavior. While acknowledging the important and good work that is done by the Unite Faith Workers' Branch, it is therefore central to our position that it must concurrently recognised that, alongside this good work, this is an organisation that over a number of years has had serious problems and has hurt and harmed various members. In this context I refer the reader back to my secretary report in the introduction to this book in which I expressesed serious concerns about alleged institutional racism and sectarianism within the Unite Faith Workers' Branch, and the very strong sentiments they have evoked among a number of Black, Asian and ethnic minority and non-Christian members. It will become apparent from this discussion that the problems of the Unite Faith Workers' Branch have been "chronic" and longstanding in a number of areas.

So, we raise concerns and complaints. The Branch is an imperfect organisation, and aims to foster a culture which actively defends and supports the freedom of Members to express concerns and criticisms within the limits of acceptable speech set out in the Unite rule book, and of listening and responding effectively to such concerns and criticisms. It is the duty of officers and members to raise concerns where they believe that someone's safety, care or well-being is being compromised by the practice of colleagues, or by those in authority, or by the systems, policies or procedures with which they are expected to work. We must encourage and support the development of a culture in which members can raise concerns openly and honestly without fear of intimidation. We therefore wish to challenge officials of Unite the Union.

This brings us to the idea of mediation. Members of the Faith Workers' Executive Committee were required to enter into a process of mediation with Unite officials as this would inform the union's review of branch structures. I had severe misgivings as to whether we should have participated in this process given that the likely outcomes would not promote equality or any other trade union values. However, the idea was to provide a space to express views from our own observations and experience, and for us to seek a constructive way forward. I was getting that sinking feeling when you just know things are not what other people claim them to be. The mediators, and there were two of these had all the right credentials but what was their motivation? I had to just go along with this even if it felt like watching the wet paint dry on a sham process. The mediators would claim their independence as impartial agents, attempting to do their best to mediate the ongoing disputes within the Faith Workers' Branch. Maybe they believed it themselves that they were only there to reform the branch structures and standing orders in a way that encourages greater equality, diversity and transparency. If you believed that you would believe anything. I did not believe that two mediators paid by Unite could be so genuine. This section of the book give clarity to why I felt the whole thing was a sham.

So, what were the terms of reference for this review? What was the brief for these impartial reviewers? And did they understand the situation into which they would be working? They had been told that there were two sides to a dispute within the Faith Workers' Branch. The newly created workplace groupings and members who are concerned by what they allege is the inherent discrimination within the Union's structures which is exploited by the Christian clergy who dominate the Branch. On the other side is a majority membership who are upset and angered by what they perceive as the constant depiction of any act which is done or undertaken by or for the majority as discriminatory, colonialist, racist and in general derogatory terms because it is not in accordance with the wishes and views of the minority. Clearly both groups and those in between would agree on one thing, namely the branch is not operating properly. Thus, there would be agreement about dysfunctionality at the core of how the branch operates and the dysfunctionality is totally against the grain of what trade unionism is all about. However, the meditators failed to convene a meeting of the full Executive Committee. The mediators were aware that the Faith Workers' Branch Executive Committee meetings had continued to operate and take decisions online. The discussion at meetings was entirely internally focused on disputes concerning minutes and previous decisions regarding the structures, remit of the Branch Executive Committee and further disputes around roles and actions of Branch Executive Committee members. They also picked up the challenges of organising effective branch meetings during the global COVID-19 pandemic. They were so sharp.

So, the mediators were asked to explore the most suitable structure for the Branch and its Executive Committee with a view to accommodating the position of all faiths and which properly satisfies the Union's commitment to equality and the law. A great idea in principle but what would be the practical steps in progressing this? They were also asked to provide clear and defined roles for the office holders in both Branch and Workplace Groupings. They never delivered on this and division within the branch became worse as a result of their intervention. They also failed during the mediation process to provide clear requirements for recognition and membership of the workplace groupings and their place in the Union structure. A code of conduct for branch members in their dealings with each other and externally was not put forward during the mediation process I was part of.

The mediators start with some wide speculations as to possible ways forward. Firstly, it was suggested that the branch could be disbanded and we become some kind of informal gathering that met once or twice a year. So, the national branch would disappear other than that the national union would keep operating the helpline and utilise people who would invest time in running that. They didn't seem to realise the helpline was staffed by local volunteers independently of Unite and its London office. They then suggested another option was to establish a Church of England branch and abolish workplace groupings. I guess this was to shock us into agreeing something they had been planning but were not going to share it with us yet. I perceived this as dishonest and a cheap tactic.

They went on to say that nothing had been decided and that the purpose of having this meeting was to hear our views, so that they could reflect on that before producing any draft proposals. I did not believe them. They also felt that there should be a review or reflection on any proposals that were to be put forward after three years, to see if they actually work in practice and to make any necessary tweaks at that stage. They also put forward the idea of an equality and a policy committee. The equality committee would sit under the equality officer and would allow for a diverse range of backgrounds to be represented and to have an advisory input. This is particularly interesting as the equality's role had been inactive for some time. They identified the role here to be about race, religion and disability, and to deal with those issues in such a way as to ensure everyone where possible were catered for. The mediators had heard some concerns about members not being engaged in the branch, so this committee would exist to look at common issues such as say minimum wage, discrimination, bullying and harassment. Any member would be able to join and they would then be able to put forward policies to the branch committee for the committee to decide on. The meditators had thought long and hard about the best way forward for the Executive Committee to guarantee diversity. When looking at positive action under the Equality Act, their starting point is that this is a discretionary thing and there is no obligation on a union or employer or anybody to implement positive action. They then looked at whether there is actually a disadvantaged group or a group who is not represented proportionately, and if not, why they are not represented. However, they did not have any information on that and so there was a problem there in terms of being able to implement any action at all. At this stage in the process the mediators were happy with the idea for having vice chairs from the exiting faith groups. They felt that co-option is the way forward here but with additional safeguards. So, you would have the six elected officers required by the rules and then you could have up to six further members of the committee co-opted on. It should not be just a case of existing members adding people into the committee who they know. The committee should invite expressions of interest and these should be looked at to determine who should join. This process should then be overseen by an external Unite officer, ideally someone who has not had involvement in any of the disputes or issues that have arisen so far.

The mediators also felt that there was a need for a communications officer. They wanted someone internally nominated once the branch committee has been formed, to deal with communications, newsletter and social media and the like. And when anything needs to be sent out on behalf of the branch, particularly if it is controversial, this would need to be agreed between the communications officer, the secretary and the chair. This should prevent people sending out messages on behalf of the branch without discussion. In terms of engagement with members, the mediators had heard that there are issues with not many members attending meetings when they are moving around the country. So, they wanted the meetings to take place somewhere centrally, whether London or Birmingham, somewhere with good union resources. The meeting could then be livestreamed out to members around the country so that they can at least watch and perhaps participate. The policy and equality committees should all be on Zoom to allow engagement from members. On training for representatives, the mediators agreed that this should not just be Christian-focused or office-holder-focused and it should include elements from other religions so that reps have some idea of the background when they are asked to help members.

Having listened carefully to the opening comments from the mediators I had to ask myself if the things they were say were the vital questions for the Faith Workers' Branch. I had been involved with this organisation for over twenty-five years. So, were they talking about the same organisation? Was their tentative proposal really related to us or was this just thrown at us to soften us up for an already-agreed programme from the head office which would be imposed on the branch at a later date? Certainly, the mediators seemed to be saying that the branch was unviable in its present form and there was a lot of talk about communications officers. Now if my position as secretary hadn't been undermined in the first place, I would be coordinating that communication. This felt like a pre-report, with mediators talking about lines of communication but did not address the issue of relationship between the Branch and Executive Committee and the unite officers as there have been massive problems in communication with Unite, particularly with the region. The mediators seemed to be unaware of conflicts between the branch and Unite officers or so they said. There was an enormous problem between us and the Unite office, particularly with London region where the branch is based.

So, what about the review of the Faith Workers' Branch of Unite the Union? Meditators in their own way had to acknowledged that the branch was dominated by White Anglicans and Methodists who were becoming very uncomfortable with those of other faith groups. With the current structure, there is an issue of Church of England members having a lot of power and being able to tell members from other groups what to do. To overcome that, the meditators suggested we have a change in the structure of the branch as a whole so that you have a skeleton branch committee of only the four requisite elected officers of chair, vice chair, secretary and treasurer who could decide on things like engagement with the wider union, trades union congress meetings, the newsletter but the real power goes to the workplace groupings and they can decide what they want to do for their members. The mediators claimed that they had not thought about this in detail.

It is interesting that an Equalities officer was not included. This could be because this work had been neglected during the triennial even though others were willing to take this key role on. The mediator's proposal did not go down too well for Muhammad Al-Hussaini and myself as this alternative structure confirms exactly what we had been saying in our previous discussions. They want to create a core group, a super Executive Committee that makes all the decisions; this is what we are complaining about. It is crucial to this that we get the relationship between Branch and Executive Committee right. We need to be very clear what decisions are made at branch level, bearing in mind there is a much bigger range of people turning up there which is very different from the Executive Committee. This proposal would marginalise under-represented groups and exclude them from the Executive Committee. It puts forward the idea of allocating even more resources to the White majority who are Anglicans and Methodists. Resources allocation on this basis seems contrary to our understanding of Union values which is why we wanted protected status on the position of vice chairs. What we need is a unitary Faith Workers' Branch, which is multi-faith and multi-racial in governance where powers are shared and decisions are not made without the minority view.

I wanted the mediators to accept that we are the people who are being discriminated against and had offered concrete examples of situations and decisions as evidence. It was for them now to know, where we go with that. It was very clear to me that at this point they had no clear direction. They were happier with admin processes and procedures than the wider vision of trade unionism and equality. There was now a lot of pious talk of all the people of the branch coming with us to change a few standing orders. The meditators wanted to accommodate as many views as possible on the premise that there is no racism and no discrimination and that people will be treated fairly and squarely. So how naive can you possibly be? They felt that there was no point in changing standing orders if there were friction within the branch. As far as I am concerned, this friction they are talking about is the result of racism and they should own it. They did not have anything to suggest with regard to how workplace groupings were to be represented on the Executive Committee although they frequently confused the Executive Committee with the Branch meeting which kind of suggests they did not really understand the structures they were reviewing. Clearly it is the branch meeting that should recognise workplace groupings as it includes ordinary members who may also want to put representatives from those groupings on to the Executive Committee. The Executive Committee already had too much power and this would be another way of making it accountable to the membership.

So, what was in the mediator's Final Report? They now came clean as to how they saw the reordering of the Faith Workers' Branch and work place groupings within that structure. They talked about a lot of other things too which were not part of the mediation process I attended. I refer here to recommendations about branch membership including work place groupings, representation and elections, new standing orders including finance policy, media and communications, a code of conduct, protection of freedom to raise concerns, institutional bullying, a dedicated officer to be assigned to the branch, and members of the Executive Committee should undergo diversity and equality training. I can only assume they talked about this with the White majority group. So, I am going to treat these later additions as irrelevant to the purpose of this book. What is important is that they now wanted an Executive Committee of six elected officers to include chair, a vice chair who would also have the title of 'minorities officer' or 'organizing officer for minority faiths', secretary, treasurer, communications officer, equalities officer. Presumably the vice-chair would now have responsibility for helping people the Equalities officer had not been able to reach like members working for faith organisations which are not represented on the Executive Committee. All this we are told would give focus to the importance of diversity of recruitment in the branch. They also felt that it would reduce the perception of institutional racism in the branch. This has to be put alongside their view on co-option which is to limit this option on the grounds it might lead to favoritism for a particular faith. They also wanted to devolve more power to workplace groupings as this would help reduce internal conflicts. The idea here would be to limit the Executive Committee function to recruiting new members and supporting workplace groupings. They would do this by considering policy-related proposals from a newly created policy and equality committee, dealing with finances, and engagement with the wider union structures. The policy and a equality committee would have no Executive Committee powers but would be an open forum for members and chaired by the minorities officer from the Executive Committee. So rather than allowing a reprehensive from a work place group to be on the Executive Committee they will have a seat on an ineffective policy group that anyone can join. Yes, I get the measure of this marginalisation only too clearly. We are told the purpose of this advisory committee will be to discuss common issues that are of widespread application. What is meant by that? Who can say? We are also told that these meetings should take place via Zoom because this is a national branch and Unite can't afford to pay expenses for members traveling some distance.

The final report gave some discussion as to whether the Executive Committee was bound by collective decision-making. They took the view that the six elected officers could form a committee within a committee to make day-to-day decisions without recourse to the wider Executive Committee. This had not been the custom of the branch before this triennial. However, when I was secretary such a group had formed involving the acting chair, vice chair and treasure with the full backing of Unite officers. We are now told that certain officers have more authority than others. We now have a hierarchy of committee members with chair, vice, secretary, treasurer and equalities officer at the top. They are followed by other elected members of the Executive Committee and the co-co-opted members of the committee are at the bottom. In that context we are told that it was appropriate for the acting chair to make decisions affecting the branch without reverting to the entire committee. I felt very strongly as did my colleagues from the Muslim and Hindu workplace groupings that decisions should be made by the Executive Committee as a whole. In their wisdom the mediators came to the conclusion that controversial decisions would require more consultation and that such decisions should be made by the full Executive Committee. What they don't say is who decides when a decision should be defined as controversial.

This chapter has tried to exposed the power politics of a trade union system that imposed a mediation process on the Faith Worker Branch which led to a review of its structures. The crucial Unite recommendations have brought about further marginalisation of the very people union values would claim to want to support. So, what has gone wrong here? The Committee within a committee approach will not promote ethnic and multi faith diversity. This committee is likely to be dominated by White majority Christians even if its minority officer was of a different ethnicity and faith. To my mind the Executive Committee needs to be expanded to include a much larger range of people from the membership and the best way of doing this at this present time is through co-options and the appointment of vice chairs drawn equally from the faith groups.

Chapter Four

Defining Black and Asian Identities and Their Theology of Context

THE PURPOSE OF THIS chapter is to draw together various themes from previous chapters that, in one way or another, give focus to the harsh reality of violence suffered by Black and Asian members as the marginalised other in a White dominated trade union movement. I want to implicitly establish a relationship between Christianity and Whiteness within the normalcy of what may be called Protestantism. In this chapter, I will try to understand the role of Protestantism in defining non-White identities. I ask if there is an ideological foundation for slavery or should this phenomenon be seen as purely economic in origin? I will seek to understand the role of Christianity in defining Black identities by exploring the possibility that the religious conflict between British Protestants and European Catholics dating back to the sixteenth century laid the foundation for later conflicts involving indigenous UK populations and those seen as outsiders.

Blackness and the Christian Tradition

Whoever controls the images of a people or a culture is crucial to the domination and identity of that people or culture. The images of Black people have been largely shaped, controlled, and nourished by beliefs about Blackness within the dominant cultural groups of Europe and America.[1]

Robert Hood, the author of the above quotation gives the frame of analysis and the starting point for our discussion of Blackness. Hood seeks to show that the result has been a growing consistency of oppression at all levels of human activity and condition so far as Black people are concerned. The degradation of Black people is constantly interpreted as natural and as just outcomes for their inadequacies. Thus, the state of Black people is seen as their problem, internal to their God-given createdness. White people are therefore safely exonerated, positively invited to remain aloof, and not to change the *status quo*. Any Black person in history who did manage to achieve at a public level either has their Blackness hidden from recorded history or were themselves expunged from the records.

Hood explains and proves that the negativity associated with Blackness has long and deep roots going back way beyond the fifteenth-century slave trade. The Greeks made cultural appraisals of Black people based upon their strangeness, expressed in the word 'barbarian', which was an onomatopoeia for the incoherence of foreign tongues.[2] The Romans added a dimension of ethnicity to this; they despised Africans as lazy, incapable of being good soldiers. The Christians introduced the moral and metaphysical category of the inferiority of Blackness via the polarity of the struggle between light and darkness; the devil was reinterpreted as a creature of sin and evil and had to be Black because of this polar paradigm. These mythic dimensions had great power in the Western psyche. Hood also explains very clearly the parallel negativity of the Western tradition of the sensuality of the exotic. Bacchus, satyrs, other such creations of classical mythology, were often presented in Negroid form. Their origins were ascribed to Africa.[3] This carnality of Blackness was perpetuated in Jewish and Christian thought, particularly after more frequent contact between Europe and Africa began. This continued as a strong theme and continues to have its

1. Hood, *Begrimed and Black*, 181.
2. Hood, *Begrimed and Black*, 29.
3. Hood, *Begrimed and Black*, 27.

influence today.[4] The strongly public, civic model of Christianity in later times has led to the co-option of the faith into preserving the *status quo*. This has prevented the challenge that can be presented by more open debates to the diminution of the church. The church has thus been strengthened as an institution by means of this enforced distancing from its true apostolic vocation. Thus, Christians have been permitted to perpetuate the myths of racial superiority and ethnic exclusivity.

Hood refers to the fact that even the etymology of the very word *Africa* is uncertain.[5] The huge, unmapped, unknown continent loomed large in European consciousness and held a fascination as well as a horror. This resulted in taxonomies to differentiate between pale Black people and deep Black people, so Arabs were not even considered African, thus allowing some discourse. It still comes as a surprise to many that Egypt is in Africa, after the Egyptology of the eighteenth and nineteenth centuries. A resurgence of this obsession with fine grades of colour was a feature of the American classifications such as mulatto, quadroon, octoroon, etc.[6]

Hood reclaims some of the positive associations with Blackness, showing how these have been expunged. He examines the implications of St. Matthew's emphasis on Jesus in Africa. He also examines the influence of the Donatist and Coptic traditions. These benign associations were swamped by the post-Gnostic dualities of light/dark, good/bad, White/Black, spiritual/carnal. Jerome began a specific and overt tradition of condemning Black as evil. By the fifth century CE, the Council of Toledo affirmed the appearance of the devil as Black, cloven-hoofed with a large phallus.[7] Blackness then became associated with the antichrist, as the Moorish invasion of Spain evinced. Presumably the assigned Whiteness of Arabs fell away as their territorial aspirations grew. Despite this, some positive traditions of Blackness persisted: the myth of Prester John as the Saviour from Ethiopia to rescue Europe from the infidel; the cult of St. Maurice, always depicted as Black, especially through northern Europe; the adoration of the Black Madonna, tapping into pre-Christian European cultic devotion to earth-mothers; the inheritance of the Magi as wisdom embodied in Blackness.

4. Jordan, *White over Black*.

5. Hood, *Begrimed and Black*, 25.

6. Hood, *Begrimed and Black*, 13.

7. Hood, *Begrimed and Black*, 89.

Hood cites the moral acrobatics that justified the European slave trader's activities that characterised both Protestant and the Roman Catholic churches. This was when the potency of the Ham myth was exploited.

> The biblical story of Ham (older spellings: Cham or Chem) has been used historically to explain the origin and natural subordination of Black cultures and peoples and the negativity of Blackness.[8]

Hood quotes the Jewish writings known as the Midrash:

> 'Since you have disabled me from doing ugly things in the Blackness of night, Canaan's children shall be born Black and ugly. Moreover, because you twisted your head around to see my nakedness, your grandchildren's hair shall be twisted into kinks, and their eyes red; again, because your lips jested at misfortune, they shall swell; and because you neglected my nakedness, they shall go naked, and their male members shall be shamefully elongated. Men of this race shall be called Negroes; their forefather Canaan commanded them to love theft and fornication, to be banded together in hatred of their masters and never to tell the truth.'[9]

Hood concludes that—

> Jewish legends put dogs, Black ravens and Black people under the same curse because they offended the taboo against cohabitation while in Noah's ark.[10]

As Hood argues, language has itself been a major vehicle for reproducing stereotypical imagery, and all languages have two basic colour-terms for black and white.[11] If a language had only three colour terms then the third would be for red. If a language had four colour terms, then it would be either yellow or green but not both. Homeric Greek had four basic colours: white, black, red, yellow.[12] This gave a very fluid set of associations: white-bright-female-tame-safe;   black-dark-dim-male-dangerous-courageous. The Greeks thought that our insides were naturally Black so 'Blackness of heart' connoted 'warm hearted', 'White-livered' is directly analogous to our 'lily livered.'[13] The Latin *negri* signified sinister and deadly and was also

---

8. Hood, *Begrimed and Black*, 155.

9. Hood, *Begrimed and Black*, 155–56.

10. Hood, *Begrimed and Black*, 156.

11. Hood, *Begrimed and Black*, 30.

12. Hood, *Begrimed and Black*, 30.

13. Hood, *Begrimed and Black*, 32.

used for complexion of North Africans.[14] Of the four humors, black bile was a sign of anger and death, melancholy. Black was associated with Hades and with Tartarus where bad deities were punished, a place of no wind and a pit where Zeus threw Chronos, his father.[15]

• • •

By the first century BCE Latin had white, black, red, yellow, green, blue. For many poets, White = divinity and good luck; Black = dread and bad luck. The Fates were described as *candidate's sorores*, White Sisters, when they brought good luck and as *sorores nigrae* when they brought misery.[16] New Testament Greek retained the Latin word to describe dark/Black Christians (Acts 13:1), 'Simeon who was called Niger'. Latin intellectuals adopted Greek cosmology and anthropology: a flat earth, at one end the frozen north, home of savage Irish, Hyperborean and British; the south which was hot and the home of Black people, Ethiopians and Numidians, who were all Black because of the sun, had shrilled voices, bow legs, a blood deficiency and made poor soldiers. The Egyptians were kept in a class of their own.[17]

According to Hood there was uncertainty from the earliest times in Europe about the origins and identifies of Black cultures. Satyrs were fabled creatures of Greek antiquity. They were known for their lust and fertility. They first appear in literature in the sixth century BCE. Extant sculptures stress their Negroid features and large genitals.[18] In the King James Version of the Bible the word 'satyr' is used for *se'irim*, hairy demons of Hebrew mythology thought to occupy wasteland (Lev 17:7). Some Greek writers thought satyrs originated from Africa.[19] In the New Testament there are references to people from Africa.[20] Egypt was potent in the Jewish tradition used by the writer of St. Matthew's Gospel and strongly associated with Jesus as a sign of delivery.[21] This was developed from the Jewish salvation history. At the time of the New Testament there were many Jews living in Egypt. *The Septuagint* (the Greek version of the Jewish Bible) was written

14. Hood, *Begrimed and Black*, 33.

15. Hood, *Begrimed and Black*, 34.

16. Hood, *Begrimed and Black*, 38.

17. Hood, *Begrimed and Black*, 39.

18. Hood, *Begrimed and Black*, 27

19. Hood, *Begrimed and Black*, 27–28.

20. Hood, *Begrimed and Black*, 46–47.

21. Hood, *Begrimed and Black*, 49.

there. Egypt had become a place friendly to Jews. Egypt's astrology was widely influential at the time of the writing of the Gospels. Matthew could well have known that it was believed that the spring equinox had moved from Aries to Pisces, causing great public anxiety. Virgil had said that this event signified the advent of a new divinity.[22] In a fresco from the tomb in the valley of the Kings, 1320–1200 BCE, four branches of humankind are depicted: red, dark brown, light brown and Black standing for Egyptians, Asiatics, Nubians and Libyans.[23] Egypt was the gateway to Africa for the Mediterranean cultures. Ethiopia is the other area of Africa known and referred to in the New Testament.[24] Homer had introduced Ethiopia to European culture as a mythical place.[25] Egypt and Ethiopia became significant centres of Christianity. Early pictures and images portray the Virgin Mary and the infant Jesus as Black with African features. Possibly the early church must have believed Jesus and his mother to be Ethiopian.

Gay Byron acknowledges *Begrimed and Black* as the first comprehensive analysis of the role of Christianity in defining Black identities with the Christian tradition.[26] However the point is made that Hood was not a biblical scholar but an historian and that his identification of ancient sources to demonstrate racial bias in the Christian literature does not take into account the many and varied rhetorical functions of this material.[27] Byron's argument is that Hood does not provide an adequate methodological framework to interpret the presence Blackness in Greco-Roman antiquity and neglects many of the gender-related issues which can be identified in the material he uses. It is this gap in the academic literature that Byron acknowledges as the starting point for her work in providing a systematic gender-based analysis of the position of Black women[28]

• • •

Byron categorises references to ethnicity within Greco-Roman literature by focusing upon their rhetorical functions.[29] Thus a taxonomy of rhetoric

22. Hood, *Begrimed and Black*, 52.

23. Hood, *Begrimed and Black*, 55.

24. Hood, *Begrimed and Black*, 57.

25. Hood, *Begrimed and Black*, 58.

26. Byron, *Begrimed and Black*, 7–8.

27. Byron, *Symbolic Blackness and Ethnic Difference*, 8.

28. Byron, *Symbolic Blackness and Ethnic Difference*, 8.

29. Byron, *Symbolic Blackness and Ethnic Difference*, 29.

demonstrates that Christian writers were influences by the cultural values of their day and that language has an important role in giving shape to those understandings. The rhetorical categories within non-Christian literature include geopolitical identification, moral-spiritual characterisation, and descriptive differentiation. A fourth category of Christian self-definition is also utilised to show how Christian writers adapted the prevailing rhetoric and put their own slant upon the process of othering ethnic groups.[30] These are categories of difference within the literature and from which a framework for interpretation is constructed. Thus, geographical references to Egypt and Ethiopia become geopolitical identifications with Egyptians and Ethiopians.

Whiteness and Protestant tradition

Moving from the founding times of the Christian faith to the founding time of the Protestant tradition, racism and the exploitation of 'inferior peoples' did not, however occur only at a great distance from England. As Michael Hetchter[31] has argued, colonialism was not restricted to those parts of the world subjected to nineteenth century overseas imperialism. Ireland can be seen as an example of internal colonialism not only because its history bears many similarities with overseas colonies, but because, to this day, we can identity a political system containing core and peripheral groups which are mediated by a metropolitan central government. The characteristics of periphery/core relations of production are as follows:

- commerce and trade among members of the periphery tend to be monopolised by members of the core;

- bankers, managers, and entrepreneurs tend to be recruited from the core;

- the colonial economy rests on a single primary export and economic dependence of the periphery on the core is reinforced through judicial, political, and military measure;

- There is migration and mobility of peripheral workers in response to price fluctuations of exported primary products.

---

30. Byron, *Symbolic Blackness and Ethnic Difference*, 30.

31. Hetchter, *Internal Colonialism*.

According to the internal colonial model, the superordinate group or core seeks to stabilise and monopolises its advantages by regulating the allocation of social roles and hence the promotion of a stratification system which benefits the core. The pattern of development in the periphery is dependent upon and complementary to that of the core. Furthermore, industrialisation at the periphery is specialised for the purpose of export.[32] According to the internal colonial model, there is national discrimination on the basis of language, religion, or other cultural forms. In order to evaluate the role of racist ideology in Britain's colonialisation of Ireland, we must try to understand the wider social and cultural context of the prevailing attitudes in England concerning the perceived racial differences between people of English and Irish origin. We need to examine the political as well as the social psychological significance of the way in which the English have constructed stereotypes of Irish culture.

Anti-Irish racism has existed in this country as long as England's involvement with Ireland. As early as the twelfth century, English writers like Giraldus Cambrensis in their writings treated the Irish as a lesser form of life, beginning a tradition that has continued. By the end of the sixteenth century, the English image of the Irish was that of an ignorant, animal-like savage. In Victorian England anti-Irish racism flourished, particularly amongst members of the English ruling class. Benjamin Disraeli described the Irish as 'a wild, reckless, indolent, uncertain and idolatrous race'.[33] Whilst Lord Salisbury claimed, in a speech to the National Union of Conservative and Constitutional Association at St. James Hall in May 1886, that the Irish were 'like Hottentots and other races incapable of self-government'.[34] Leading historians and academics helped the politicians whip up anti-Irish racism, claiming that Ireland was a land of superstitious savages.

Clearly, in the consolidation of nineteenth-century English ethnicity, the reproduction of racist imagery went beyond the symbolism of African identities, but at the same time the range of racist reference helped to normalise the central ideology of 'race' as salient and significant. These racial myths and stereotypes have been built on the need to reinforce English and later British supremacy. However, the role which racist ideology played in Britain's colonialisation of Ireland can be related directly to the significance of Protestantism as an agent of economic, political, and social exclusion.

32. Hetchter, *Internal Colonialism*, 32.

33. Curtis, *Anglo-Saxons and Celts*, 150–51.

34. Curtis, *Anglo-Saxons and Celts*, 102–3.

The division of the Irish working class in the six northern counties started with the migration of English and Scottish Protestants to Ireland in the sixteenth and seventeenth centuries, with this group receiving land concessions and favorable tenancies. They became a significant but troublesome ally of the English state and as custodians of Protestantism they found themselves in opposition to the Roman Catholic population. At the end of the eighteenth century, Protestant tenants and their landlords were locked in conflict with Roman Catholic workers who desired independence. And in the nineteenth and early twentieth centuries, Loyalist workers in collaboration with their employers continued to oppose self-determination.

Protestantism was equally important in linking Scotland to England and Wales by the Act of Union in 1707. According to Linda Colley, it was Protestantism that forged these countries together into one nation. It was through this denominational Christian tradition that the British people made sense of the world in which they lived. In other words, it determined their politics. Protestantism told the British that they were not only different from but also superior to their European neighbours who embraced Roman Catholicism. Colley comments that this Protestantism was 'uncompromising'.[35] The main enemy was Catholic France with whom Britain was often at war.

So why did this happen? Why did the United Kingdom come into existence? Why did the Scots, Welsh, and English accept one Parliament, a system of free trade in which all paid the same taxes and custom duties and, above all, one Protestant ruler? The United Kingdom was not a unity of absorption. All three countries maintained their separate identities, such as they were, and, in the case of Wales, its own language still official to this day. However within each country there was no uniformity or monolithic system of custom and organisation. One thing that did unite all three countries was their commitment to a Protestant worldview that would, by the end of the seventeenth century, exclude Roman Catholics from the institutions of government. They could not vote or enter Parliament. The Protestant State considered them to be likely traitors. Catholics were treated with suspicion and contempt while Protestant dissenters were allowed a measure of religious and political freedom. Great Britain was a Protestant polity that propagated anti-Catholicism.

Anti-Catholic propaganda was not restricted to the pulpit. This ideology was disseminated through the fast-growing printing industry that was

35. Colley, *Britons*.

producing almanacs and newspaper. Popular literature, taking advantage of higher literacy, had been instrumental in the ideological battle against Catholicism. By recounting an exclusively Protestant version of their history, almanacs told the British who they were and their place in the order of things. Colley draws our attention to the publication of John Foxe's *Book of Martyrs*[36] that informed its readers of the persecution of Protestants during the reign of Queen Mary; she also refers to John Bunyan's *Pilgrim's Progress*[37] as examples of the literature of mass Patriotism.

British Protestants believed that they were a chosen people and that their struggle with foreign Catholics in this life was somehow purposed by God in order to test their suitability for salvation in the world to come.[38] This eschatology was also realisable in this world as demonstrated by the establishment and maintenance of a Protestant monarchy. The Catholic king, James II, was forced into exile to allow his Protestant daughter, Mary, to rule jointly with her equally Protestant husband, William of Orange, in 1688.[39] Despite their obvious loyalty, they still had to proclaim publicly their allegiance to the British State by agreeing to rule in such a way as would be in keeping with the Christian gospel and Reformed Protestant religion. When Queen Anne came to the throne in 1702, she had to make a declaration against transubstantiation, as a Roman doctrine regarding the nature of the consecrated elements at Holy Communion. The Act of Settlement in 1701 excluded Catholics, or anyone married to a Catholic, from the British throne.[40] When George Lewis of Hanover became king in 1714, fifty other contenders with stronger hereditary claims were passed over because they were known Catholics.[41] The key concept was that of providence, which replaced the divine right of kings. It was a combination of providence, i.e., God's will on the one hand, and the will of the people on the other that gave life to and sustained this Protestant dynasty.

36. Colley, *Britons*, 27–28.
37. Colley, *Britons*, 28–29.
38. Colley, *Britons*, 29.
39. Colley, *Britons*, 48.
40. Colley, *Britons*, 48.
41. Colley, *Britons*, 49.

The Abolition of Slavery

So, what part did Protestantism play in the abolition of the slave trade? The irony that the nation that had profited so greatly from slavery should be the first to seek its abolition has to be put into a political and social context which includes religion as a powerful change agent. Ideas about providence, God's will for the British nation, were still strong at the beginning of the nineteenth century. Britain was the New Jerusalem and, with God's help, had kept the Catholic hordes at bay. Thus, for the British Protestants, the ending of the slave trade was an act of atonement. It also provided a timely distraction allowing the British state to deflect Chartist demands for universal suffrage.[42] Anti-slavery was also a means of uniting the nation at a time when fear of Catholic foreigners had waned after the battle of Waterloo. I am not suggesting for one moment that the British embraced anti-slavery out of the goodness of their White liberal hearts, although the sincere contributions of notable campaigners such as Wilberforce cannot be denied. Rather, anti-slavery became another method of British supremacy. The British could now teach the world about freedom.

So how quickly did anti-slavery become the accepted policy in the Church of England? At the beginning of the eighteenth century, the attitude of the Church of England towards the institution of slavery was one of toleration. In 1727 the Bishop of London, Thomas Sherlock, who had responsibility for the plantations, set out the official church line by claiming that the Christian gospel would not interfere with civil property.[43] Church leaders assured the planters that the reception of their slaves into the established church would not impede their work or affect their status and that baptism was not being offered to them as a ideological preparation to earthly freedom. The freedom on offer to them was freedom from their sins, not freedom from the sins of their masters.

The Church of England then was presented to the slave owners as a safe institution that would not undermine business interests. This approach was in stark contrast with that of other religious groups, such as the Quakers, who some slave masters perceived as stirring up the slaves and inciting them to rebellion. George Fox's controversial visit to Barbados in 1671 was treated with great suspicion. Fox preached that Christ had died for all people, including his newfound congregation who were slaves. What Fox had actually

42. Colley, *Briton*, 381.
43. Fryer, *Staying Power*, 146.

preached according to Fryer was not rebellion but rather the status quo. Thus, using Fox's own words, he preached "justice, sobriety, Temperance, Chastity and Piety, and to be subject to their masters and Governors."[44]

So why then did the planters trust the Church of England not to challenge what was for them a lucrative industry? Up until the great crisis of consciousness awakened by Wilberforce and others, the Church of England had no difficulty in providing justifications for the slave trade. Church leaders had for some time claimed that slavery was the will of God and that there was no conflict between the Christian gospel and the principle that one person could own and dispose of another. The pro-slavery cleric Raymond Harris published a book dedicated to the mayor and aldermen of the city of Liverpool to which are added scriptural directions for the proper treatment of slaves claiming biblical support for the institution of slavery.[45] The line of argument was simple and, at times, simplistic. Taking text far from context, Harris seeks to show that God condoned slavery in the books of the Old Testament. Having established this important principle, there was no reason to believe that God had changed his mind with regard to Negro slavery four or five thousand years later. Granville Sharp, who in his essay 'Just Limitation of Slavery in the Laws of God' written a decade before Harris, had already pointed out that biblical support for slavery was restricted to seven heathen nations who were in direct opposition to the Israelites and only then for a limited period of time. The Israelites were charged to love the stranger, as they were themselves strangers in the land of Egypt.[46]

Harris also interprets the Christian doctrine of 'love thy neighbour' as support for the slave trade. He argues thus: The Christian slave master could not implement this principle unless

> with the same tenderness, justice and humanity as he would have his slave behave to him were the slave the master and he himself the slave.[47]

And for the same reason the slave could not realise this principle unless they served their master—

---

44. Fryer, *Staying Power*, 147.

45. Harris, *Scriptural Researches on the Licitness of the Slave-Trade.*

46. Sharp, *Essays.*

47. Gratus, *Great White Lie*, 142.

with the same fidelity, submission and respect that he would expect from his master were the latter his slave and himself the master.[48]

Sharp, in his essay 'Self-Love', dismissed such propositions as contrary to the gospel of Christ. He comments thus:

> slavery is absolutely inconsistent with Christianity because we cannot say of any slaveholder that he doth to another what he would have done to himself. For he is continually exacting involuntary labour from the other without wages which he would think monstrously unjust were he himself the sufferer.[49]

The Church of England, in the early eighteenth century, was slow to embrace anti-slavery. It was, however, concerned that slaves should be baptised and allowed to attend Sunday services. This was the only demand that the church would make upon the planters. The missionary work of the church was carried out by the Society for the Propagation of the Gospel, an organisation that owned plantations and slaves in Barbados. Colley concludes that, although slavery could be seen as an obstacle to free trade, it was ended in the UK and the West Indian colonies not for economic reason or through fear of a slave uprising but because the British ruling elite had had enough. Finally, their consciences had got the better of them, albeit for fear of God's wrath. The British State, however, did not feel so disgusted by its past record that it gave up its empire.

So, what were the economic factors which were favorable to abolition? Racialised relations of production within capitalism have always been economic. But can we say that slavery was an economic system of previously racially unclassified exploitation; that slavery only brought about racism when racial meaning was attached to it? According to Eric Williams, 'Slavery was not born of racism: rather, racism was the consequence of slavery'.[50] Thus racism did not cause slavery, but slavery did cause racism. For Williams, slavery in the Caribbean has been too narrowly defined as Black slavery and he notes that the initial use of Indian slaves in the New England colonies was followed by that of the poor White, many of whom were indentured servants. By the end of the seventeenth century, the British economy was less concerned with the accumulation of precious metals than with the development of industry and exports. The focus was upon

48. Gratus, *Great White Lie*, 142

49. Sharp, *Essays*, 33.

50. Williams, *Capitalism & Slavery*, 7.

how to reduce costs in order to compete with other countries. A large population made it possible to pay low wages. The position of White servants in the colonies became worse. The plantation owners had less interest in the welfare of White servants than in Black slaves because the former were only temporarily bound by the conditions of the contract.

• • •

So, was the White servant a slave also? According to Williams, they were not. There were important differences of status between indentured servants and Negro slaves. The servant's loss of liberty was for a specified period of time; a slave was a slave for life. The status of a servant was not passed on to their children; the children of Black slaves took the status of their mother. The servant had some rights that were to be found in a legal contract. Thus the employer never had complete control over their person and liberty as they did over Negro slaves. The institution of White servitude had a number of serious disadvantages. There was a problem of supply. There just were not enough servants to replace those who had served their term. Those that had served their term wanted land at the end of their contract. Some left before completing their contract. All this made labour expensive. So, the origin of Black slavery was not racial but economic. Compared with Indian and White labour, so-called Negro slavery was superior on account of its cheapness. The negative beliefs that attribute significance to biological characteristics were later rationalisations to justify a course of action directed by economic considerations that took place within a given historical context. The White planters did not prefer Black slaves to White because somehow, they perceived the former as sub-human, at least not in the first instance. What they perceived was profits. They did not care what colour the labour was as long so it produced those profits.

There is a strong argument that the success of the anti-slavery movement was based on the greater economics of non-slave sugar production that took place outside of the Caribbean. However, to suggest that the slave owners were colourblind in their pursuit of economic gain would seem to ignore the role played by religious ideology and racialisation processes. According to Winthrop D. Jordan, slavery required *difference* that was provided by the enslavement of Africans.[51] It was not purely economic factors and the need for cheap labour that singled out the Negro for degradation. Jordan makes the point that Africans were not only visibly different from

51. Jordan, *White over Black*.

the English but that they were perceived by the latter to be set apart by religious conditions also. Englishness and Christianity were one and the same for the English so the African was a clear example of heathenism. The English could now define themselves as Christian in relation to the heathen since heathenism was the negation of a Christian life style. Thus, the heathen had helped the English to define themselves by being what the English were not. However, Christianity as doctrine had required the English to convert the African to be what the English were. The missionary imperative to convert was in direct conflict with the status quo that was a valuable focal point for self-definition. As it turned out, the English did little to resolve this conflict and missionary activity was relatively slow to get started.

Christianity is more than a set of doctrines. In the context of African slavery, Christianity functioned as a heritage that guided the reaction of Englishness toward the Negro. Christianity told the English that all people were made in the image of God but it also told them that God was an Englishman. Thus, by implication, the Negro was a heathen and, as such, represented a separate category of person. According to Jordan, the Protestantism of English Christianity, with its emphasis on individualism, encouraged this ambivalence towards the Negro and goes some way in explaining why there was no rush in the early days of contact to bring them into the Christian fold. Jordan's argument is that this religious difference was racialised in such as way as to link Blackness to barbarity. Thus, following Jordan, we can argue that Black slavery was racial slavery with religious implications. By the eighteenth century, Negro slaves were referred to as Black people or Africans and the slave owners were no longer Christian but English or White. These changes in terminology, suggesting a decline in religious culture in favour of secular nationality, represented minor adjustments within the concept of racial difference. Heathenism by itself was never the criterion upon which enslavement took place, it was only a characteristic. Heathenism could be changed by Baptism and by conversion to the Christian faith. Heathenism was rather an attribute of the Negro to be confused with other attributes in order to make racial slavery self-explanatory.

Racial Prejudice and Church Membership

The next section of this chapter draws upon the legacy of slavery and will seek to clarify the pattern of representations of the other to be found in contemporary British society which convey racial prejudice and racism. This is informed by the racialisation processes which still operate in British society today. This approach has been deployed to interpret the process which sets Black and Asian people apart by attributing significance to biological characteristics such as skin colour. Thus, I am concerned with the ideological processes which extend racial meaning to a previously racially unclassified relationship. Many researchers have defined racism as those beliefs and arguments which give rise to the identification of a negatively evaluated racial category. Thus, racism refers to those negative beliefs held by one group which identify and set apart another by attributing significance to some biological or other in inherent characteristic which it is said to possess. The word 'inherent' is used to indicate that although the characteristics in question may not be biologically based it is perceived as if it were. The important thing here is that the possession of the characteristics is thought to be determined. Institutional racial discrimination originates in the operation of established and respected forces and values in society. To understand the concept of institutionalised racism we must not only look to the racist belief system which operates in society but accept the possibility that certain institutions through a system of sub cultures are able to amplify these values. Thus, the actions of policymakers and institutional functionaries can have an adverse impact on racial groups even when race is not mentioned or when there is no intention to discriminate.

• • •

So, what is the relationship between racial prejudice and church membership? What is the twentieth-century historical background? By far the majority of studies concerning the relationship between racial prejudice and religion relates especially to the American situation. They show that the relation between racial prejudice and religion, behaviour and values is one in which churchgoers are more racially prejudiced than non-churchgoers. However, when the researchers use terms such as 'intrinsic'[52] and 'committed' to describe religious orientation, then distinctions can be made between committed Christians who go to church out of conviction and conventional churchgoers who attendance is infrequent and is motivated by social customs. Thus, conventional churchgoers may be more prejudiced than non-churchgoers; but committed Christians who attend church are no more prejudiced than non-churchgoers.

52. Allport and Ross, "Personal Religious Orientation."

The relation of religion and racial prejudice has been investigated within the European context by Bagley who discovered similar patterns in the data from English and Dutch samples.[53] According to Bagley's analysis there is

> *a major sub group in the population sample who accept religious values, but who also accept prejudiced opinions, and whose religious affiliation does not involve them in the life of their church to the extent of attending regularly, giving regularly, or having a church function.*[54]

Bagley's survey showed that racial prejudice was highest among members of the Church of England. There is a significant relationship between religiosity and racial prejudice in the United States.[55] The greater the religiosity, the greater the amount of racial prejudice to be found.[56] According to Alport and Ross, this only holds true when religion is insufficiently differentiated, that is when church membership is the only measure of religious commitment and when individuals who claim such membership are grouped together.[57] Highly committed church members were more likely to be tolerant of others because they were able to step outside the dominant value system of a racially prejudiced society. It was those church members who were less active and whose affiliation was based upon personal rather than ideological considerations, who were found to be the most prejudiced.

Gorsuch and Aleshire have reviewed a number of studies which have related measures of religious activity to measures of racial prejudice to.[58] What follows is a summary of that review. Parry using an antisemitic scale as the measure of prejudice, found the church going Protestants were less anti sematic the non-churchgoing Protestants.[59] Chein with a sample population of housewives, found that church attendance correlated negatively with prejudice among Catholics but not at all for Protestants.[60] Shinert and Ford using an Ethnocentrism scale as a measure of racial prejudice found that daily attenders at Mass were lower on the 'E' scale than non-daily

---

53. Bagley, "Relation of Religion."
54. Bagley, "Relation of Religion," 224.
55. Allport and Krammer, "Some Roots of Prejudice."
56. Rokeach, "Value Systems in Religion."
57. Allport and Ross, "Personal Religious Orientation."
58. Gorsuch and Aleshire, "Christian Faith and Prejudice."
59. Parry, "Protestants, Catholics and Prejudice."
60. Hardin et al., *Prejudice and Ethnic Relations.*

attenders.[61] Lenski used Pro/Con school integration as a measure of racial prejudice.[62] The more highly involved the individual is in church, the more likely to favour integration. By contrast, the more involved in the sub community, the more likely an individual is to favour segregation. Photiadis and Johnson used a social distance scale.[63] They found that church participation correlated with tolerance. Ragan using a population sample of White Methodist Church members, also found that persons more highly involved in the programme of the church are more tolerant than those less highly involved.[64] King and Hunt also found a relationship between attendance and intolerance.[65]

Immigrant Host Relations—A Revisit in the Context of the Racialised Other

A considerable amount of research literature investigated the presence of Black and Asian people within American society in terms of immigrant host relationships, that is the relationship between Black migrants and the indigenous White population. The analysis of such relationships has been undertaken from three major perspectives: assimilation, accommodation and pluralistic integration. Assimilation according to Robert Ezra Park is the name given to the process by which people of diverse racial origins and different cultural heritage occupy a common territory, achieve a cultural solidarity sufficient at least to sustain a national existence.[66] It is the process whereby individuals or groups of differing ethnic heritage are absorbed into the dominant culture of society. Thus, through contact with the dominant culture they gradually give up most of their own culture and take on the new cultural traits to such a degree that they become socially indistinguishable from the indigenous population. So, assimilation emphasis is the loss or modification of the foreign heritage of the immigrant group and the adoption of the language, political ideas and social customs of the host nation.

If the idea of assimilation implies social stability rather than absorption, then it can be defined in Park's terms as the actual attainment of a

---

61. Shiner and Ford, "Relation of Ethnocentric Attitudes."

62. Lenski, *Religious Factor.*

63. Photiadis and Johnson, "Orthodoxy, Church Participation, and Authoritarianism."

64. Ragan, "Attitudes of White Methodist Church Members."

65. King and Hunt, *Measuring Religious Dimensions.*

66. Park, "Sociology."

common social unity, participation and identification. Culturally, however, the concept still refers to the merging and fusion of divergent attitudes, sentiments, values and practices. If a state of full assimilation is reached when everyone shares a common culture, then, we must ask what this common culture could possibly be? Park acknowledges the unequal power relationship characteristic of the accommodation phase, but does not relate this to his concept of assimilation. There is no guarantee that this process of assimilation will result in a mutual exchange of cultures. Is it not more likely to result in the obliteration of the subordinate culture? Further, no matter how similar or divergent its culture from that of the host country, the immigrant group must decide if it wants to give up its culture or retain it. If an immigrant group decides upon the latter, they will have to defend their culture in the alien environment of the host nation. This environment is likely to be hostile because a culture usually suits the conditions, political and economic, of the country to which it is attached.

Park's ethnic cycle represent a series of supposedly analytic stages through which immigrant groups have to pass in order to achieve full participation in the common life of the host community. These stages are initial contact through competition, conflict, accommodation, and finally, assimilation. When groups of people become conscious of competition with other groups of people for goods and services, initial social contact turns into open conflict. But conflicting social and economic forces are kept in check by a moral and political order which offers accommodations and thus equilibrium is restored. The accommodation stage does not last for long because it is based upon superiority-subordination rank orders. New social forces emerge and there is a return to overt conflict. For Park, race and ethnicity, at the sociological level of analysis, are really about status groups which seek to enhance their relative position. Thus, his model of contact, conflict, accommodation, and assimilation is about identity and self-worth and is characterised by rational adjustments of activities among a plurality of interests on the basis of negotiation and reconciliation.

The principles of Park's race relations cycle were implicitly adopted by the commission which investigated the causes of the 1919 Chicago race riots under the direction of Charles S. Johnson, a Black graduate student in the department of sociology at Chicago University. This commission published his report in 1922. The riot had been precipitated by an incident at a public bathing beach at facility not generally available to Black people. Violence had also occurred at the transfer points of the street railway system.

These were located in White areas and Black people had to use them to get to work. The findings of the Commission amounted to a realisation of the central role of public opinion in the build-up of racial tension. The report recommended better policing, the control of White athletic clubs, adequate supervision of recreational facilities, and the formation of civic organisations to promote racial harmony. As far as the Commission was concerned, it was the prevailing state of public opinion which prevented Chicago from moving on to the next stage of Park's race relations cycle. Thus, a precondition to accommodation was a common moral order based upon a consensus reflected in a modified public opinion. It could be argued that a measure of accommodation has been achieved with regard to public playgrounds, where self-segregation generally prevailed, and at stores, theatres and restaurants where informal methods of exclusion were used.

Following racial tensions on the West Coast, Park, in 1923, led a team of researchers who set out to study the process by which people of Japanese origin had been incorporated into the economic life of American communities. Financial support for this project dried up a year later when the Japanese Exclusion Act of May 1924 stopped the entry of Japanese immigrants and with it the anxiety of the White middle class. The findings were predictable and more like journalism than sociology. The initial contacts of Americans and Japanese were followed by competition, accommodation and eventual assimilation. The race relations cycle was irreversible and initial contact had led to competition. Park also found that personal friendships had a part to play in lowering the barriers of segregation and caste. The children of Japanese immigrants were being Americanised and for the Park this meant assimilation.

For Franklin Frazier, the ethnic cycle does not necessarily culminate in assimilation as Park understood it.[67] The initial stage of contact was not really a social relationship at all. Without a common moral order, conflict would be bitter. Frazier's second stage represented an organised system of economic exploitation such as slavery. While in his third stage, which corresponded to Park's idea of accommodation, political control was exercised through custom and habit which included the cultivation of an 'Uncle Tom' style of leadership. Frasier's final stage, characterised by a bi-racial system of social organisation in which each race had his own set of social institutions, brakes total company with Park. Frazier describes a system of extensive amalgamation and this is not to be confused with assimilation. For Frazier,

67. Frazier, *Black Bourgeoisie*.

the Black middle class could be distinguished from the White middle class on the grounds that the former had no power base within the wider American economy. What power and influence the Black Bourgeoisie did hold was as a result of holding strategic positions within segregated institutions.

Park's race relations cycle, based as it is on the immigrant host model, underestimates the existence of racial prejudice and discrimination. It is this structural inequality which is likely to inhibit any process of assimilation. An integrated society, which has passed successfully through all the stages of Park's race relations cycle, is one in which people, regardless of their race or religion, move freely among one another sharing the same opportunities and the same public privileges and facilities on an equal basis. Thus, a fully integrated society is one in which racial discrimination does not exist. So, does Park's cycle of race relations based upon an immigrant host model represent a major reappraisal of genetics as a valid determinant of social organisation? Does it represent a decisive shift in racial thinking from biological to exclusively social explanations of human behaviour? I don't think it does and for this reason I am going to argue that the legacy to be carried over from biological thinking about race finds expression in Park's acceptance of social Darwinism. For Park the existing territorial order and the functional relations of individuals and groups are controlled by the same competition as found in the struggle for existence.[68] Park uses Darwin's terminology in his explanation of social process. Thus, it is with the unstable equilibrium characteristic of the race relations cycle that the survival of the fittest comes into its own. The succession, which refers in biology to the displacement of one species of animals by another, has been applied by Park to the movement of immigrant groups through the stages of initial social contact, competition, accommodation and assimilation. Park's cycle of race relations not only borrows from the evolutionary ideas of Darwin but incorporates typological theories which argue that in nature there are permanent and discreet racial types.

Darwinism argued that population groups were not types but closely related forms which had evolved in different climates according to natural selection and the survival of the fittest. Thus, evolution could be assisted if interbreeding populations were kept separate. Typological theories of racial variation based upon historical separateness of ancient and distinct human stocks were not necessarily superseded by the idea of geographical races which continually change as the result of the struggle for life. A

68.

commitment to a theory of racial types and racial inequality can easily be reformulated as a theory of biological change, thus drawing selectively on evolutionary ideas so as to support typological preconceptions. Clearly the word 'type' has been replaced with the term 'population group', and there are as many groups as categories invented for measuring them. Both typological theory and social Darwinism assume that there are different racial groups or categories and that they are arranged hierarchically. Clearly both theories can provide justification for racial inequality and discrimination. For the typologists, segregation is necessary in order to maintain the purity of the White 'race' and by consequence its superiority. While for the Social Darwinists, segregation is necessary to achieve this purity and superiority. Thus, racial prejudice is innate and serves a social function. The natural inclination to hate other races ensures that the fittest will survive.

Park, in discussing the Indian caste system, suggests that it is a system of hereditary class distinction that had its origins in the diversity of racial types.[69] He talks about different races in the same way as he does about different species. Thus, he used the terms 'racial stock' and 'hybrid mulatto'. Park had no difficulty in talking about racial temperament and how this might be determined by physical characteristics. Race and ethnicity are confused by Park, but it is clear that race is not an illusionary term for him, since he attaches both cultural and racial traits to what he calls races. These racial groups or types are only seen, however, in the pure form in isolation from other groups or types. Thus, the separation of races only comes to an end with the hybridisation of people which is a consequence of various stages of the race relations cycle. According to Park it is only by natural selection and inbreeding those different racial stocks are characterised by physical and cultural traits.[70] Park drew selectively on evolutionary ideas to support typological preconceptions. Different races like different species remain distinct until their pattern of association changes from symbiotic to social. However, he abandoned those aspects of the existing racial theories which view racial prejudice as a reflection of an instinctual dislike between different races. From his own knowledge of the American South, he knew that race etiquette did not reflect social distance, based on a natural instinctual dislike between races, but rather enforced it. Thus, for Park, racial prejudice is not an attribute of human beings but rather the result of the

69. Park, *Race and Culture*, 92.

70. Park, *Race and Culture*, 85.

shifting relationship between racial groups which occurs when there is a real or imaginary threat to the existing pattern of social relationships.

Park does not explicitly and systematically seek explanations of social action based on biological tenants in the way that social Darwinists did. For Park, prejudice and discrimination are socially learned, not biologically inherited. This is a crucial distinction because it renders them amenable to social intervention in ways that social Darwinism does not allow. For Park, social intervention is possible and beneficial, but for social Darwinists it is impossible in principle and thus detrimental. The discussion of the various conceptual definitions of how immigrant groups are treated or find themselves as in Park's cycle of adaptation, amalgamation and absorption is crucial to our understanding of the role of racialisation processes in defining Black and Asian identities.

So how should we conclude this chapter? The notion of racial superiority which structured the symbolic division between Black and White is a least two thousand years old. So, what is the relationship between capitalism and slavery and that of other forms of racialised oppression? It cannot be confined to the period of nineteenth-century slavery and the relationship between colonialism and racism. This is to take William's argument a stage further that slavery has been too narrowly defined. I would also agree with Jordan that slavery required difference. However, that does not refute William's claim that racism did not bring about slavery but rather slavery brought about racism. So how is racial meaning attached to previously racially unclassified situations? Clearly a nation's culture, both social and political, is the consequence of historical processes. Thus, the British feeling of racial superiority, founded upon its colonial past, has become part of UK culture. To hold and keep an empire, it was necessary to socialise people into believing that they were both a 'race' and superior to other 'races'. This is evinced in the popular slogan of *putting the great back into Britain* occasionally to be found in the tabloid press, oblivious to the geographical nature of the term 'great'.

• • •

The attempt of the Church of England during the colonial period to take politics out of Christianity is a denial of the truth. It removes it from reality and makes the assumption that it is a product of the mind only which amounts to a flat refusal to accept that Christianity is revealed in the present and subsequently can only be understood and practised in an historical context of the past. It would seem that the slave traders wanted an external, transcendent God who would allow them to oppress others while the Quakers, like George Fox, wanted an immanent God who would challenge the inner conscience. Despite the passing of the Catholic Emancipation Act in 1829, Britain remained a Protestant nation unwilling to make any major concession to Roman Catholics. Ireland had been incorporated into the UK in 1800 by an Act of Union that did nothing to reduce divisions along religious lines.

The conclusion to this discussion is not to be found exclusively in the internal colonial context of Ireland where Protestantism continues to play a vital part in maintaining British rule. It is to be found also in recognition that the concept of Whiteness as a signifier of European identity becomes increasingly more specialised and specific when applied to Englishness and is a signpost to its geographical and ecclesiastical insularity. It can be argued that England exchanged its European identity for a British identity (while maintaining its Englishness) during the colonial expansion of the nineteenth century which was also the time of missionary activity. The British colonised huge tracts of land and were not seriously challenged by any cultural cousin until the Second World War. The British Empire meant that the English were isolated and estranged from the rest of Europe, which accounts to some extent for the defensive, reactive nature to English identity through which Anglicanism had already become a repository of oppression. The British had four centuries in which to distrust Catholics who happened to be French, Spanish and Italian. In so doing, they united a kingdom of White groups who previously described themselves as English, Irish, Scottish, and Welsh. By the time Afro Caribbeans and South East Asians came to the UK in any significant numbers in the 1950s and 1960s, the British already knew how to exclude them from the institutions of White society and that included White majority churches, like the Church of England. Thus, our conclusion links this chapter to an understanding of Englishness as a cultural system, in opposition to continental Catholicism which has implications for Muslim and Hindu communities in contemporary Britain and for the whole Faith Workers' agenda. In this chapter we have been concerned with the nature of ethnic inequality and the power relationship between minority groups and the dominant culture in British society. We have tried to understand how these structural inequities have been racialised and reproduced to find their way into contemporary society and have an impact on non-White members of Unite the Union.

Conclusion

I'm Sick of It Now

Some conclusions on Englishness and English exclusivity
within the British Labour movement

I DID CONSIDER IT a privilege to serve the Faith Workers' Branch of Unite, as its treasurer and then as branch secretary. I thank the members for their trust in me as I fulfilled those roles. I came to this involvement from a social service background where I was chair of the Shop Stewards' Committee for NALGO in North London a few decades ago. I have a lifelong commitment to trade unionism and its values as active for justice and inclusivity. I resigned from Unite, the union, when it abandoned those principles. Today the Faith Workers' Branch of Unite the Union, like the Church of England, is a signifier of Englishness and English exclusivity. It is postcolonial and relies upon a historical perspective that gives focus to the idea that the natural inhabitants of the UK are White and Christian. The single British identity inherited from New Labour is superseded by a national cohesiveness which is both English and White, so questions about Englishness are also questions about Whiteness as a cultural construct—the norm turning anything connected with non-White into a category of dependence. Whiteness, therefore, has no consciousness of its own and exists appositionally to others. In this way, the notion of Englishness is used to signify privilege and turns Muslim and Hindu trade union members into outsiders. In the British Labour movement cultural Whiteness is the norm, so Anglicans and Methodists are under no pressure to conform to any other group, because they are the significant group. There are no explanations to be made either to themselves or to anyone else. This makes their position one of realised arrogance to the rest of the faith world. This clearly cannot be what their Lord and creator would want for them but how do we get them to understand this?

There is an implicit hypothesis: that the Faith Workers' Branch has been more concerned with maintaining established procedures and a narrow interpretation of the Unite Rule Book than working for justice for all its members. The relationship between these cherished structures and the Muslim and Hindu workplace groupings was determined by a political agenda which has its origin in a post-colonial understanding of the world. In this context the enlightened members of the branch found themselves in dispute with worldly authorities who eschew challenge and who did not want to change their position and focus. These resistant structures and protocols were in place and defended to maintain the status quo. The Faith Workers' Branch needed to be committed to equality as a crucial trade union value, not merely at the lip-service, rhetorical level but practically, taking concrete measures to live that inclusive and empowering life. Clearly, the old guard did not share the same view on equality. Historically they had adopted a protestant worldview which entangles them in contractionary ideas and a confusion of perspective. But more about this later.

In order to gain an understanding of institutionalised racism the trade union movement must equip itself with a knowledge of the imperial past of Britain as a nation. To hold and keep such an entity as an empire, it was necessary to socialise the British into thinking that there were racial groups and that the one they belong to was somehow superior to every other racial group. This was our focus in chapter 4. Thus, the racialised myths and stereotypes have all been built on the need to reinforce White supremacy. If the British Labour movement is to assist this so-called nation in rejecting negative images of Black and Asian people, then it must eliminate these racialised meanings from its own thinking and actions.

The concept of multi-culturalism is not always helpful and can give rise to separate provision for so-called ethnic groups and result in the isolation of Black and Asian communities from British society. The trade union movement believes it has a commitment to educate its membership and the British public and the ability to offer solutions to the problem. Yet it has failed in so many respects particularly to educate itself in the complexities of racial discrimination let alone offer advice to others. This failure to understand the influence of racism and exclusion has resulted in the identification of Black and Asian trade unionists as a problem in the British Labour movement and very much so in the Faith Workers' Branch.

So how do we engage with the origins of Whiteness? Any consideration of the origins of Whiteness in the UK will involve us in a history of those who have been marginalised in these islands for many decades. This section of my conclusion will be a very brief sketch of that history, but this history is more than mere information as it gives meaning and significance to who the marginalised are and where they are coming from. We start with Paul Gilroy who in his seminal work *There Ain't No Black in the Union Jack*[1] tells us that the politics of 'race' in the UK is not only driven by the idea of national belonging and homogeneity but relies on a confusion between race and nation to achieve its discriminatory purpose. So, statements about nation are invariably synonymous with statements about race and that has the effect of excluding Black and Asian people. It is based upon an anachronistic image of Britain as a homogenous and cohesive formation. This can be exemplified by the press response to the uprisings of 1981 where Black protest was characterised as a natural consequence of the menacing Black depictions of predatory single muggers and images of rowdy Black crowds disturbing the peace of old England. Crime was identified as Black presence in a deeply disturbing fashion through headlines such as 'Race Mob Run Riot', 'Mob Fury' and 'Riot Fury'. Suddenly that long English tradition of challenge to authority and the celebration of plurality, as encapsulated in the Church of England's tradition of independence of thought for the individual, were viewed as a threat to social order posed exclusively by out-of-control Black youths. This blurred the distinctions between real Black activism as opposed to crime.

In order to understand how Black and Asian trade unionists are presented in the press we must move the focus of our analysis to the social processes which reproduce social institutions. The racialised relations of production within capitalist societies have always been economic. Following the work of Eric Williams discussed in chapter 4 we can say that slavery was an economic system of racially unclassified exploitation. Slavery only brought about racism when racial meaning was attached to it. Thus, racism did not cause slavery but capitalism did and for its own reasons. Black and

---

1. Gilroy, *There Ain't No Black*.

Asian people in British society have limited access to the resources which wealth and favorable market position make possible. It follows therefore that any discussion of 'race', 'ethnicity' and the media must take into account the differential distribution of resources and political power.

According to van Dijk writing within a decade of the Brixton uprisings, the reproduction of racism in the British press can be analyzed at the societal macro-level; at the micro-level; and along the macro-micro dimension.[2] By the term 'reproduction', van Dijk means a dialectical interaction of principles and actual practices that form the historical continuity of a social system. At the macro level of analysis, a societal system of racism is historically reproduced when its process, rules, laws and structures remain the same. At the micro level of analysis, the repetitive practices of discrimination in everyday life form the general principles upon which the structural inequality are based. Thus, along the macro/micro dimension, socioeconomic systems are linked in continuity with cultural and cognitive systems of knowledge and belief.

At the micro level of societal reproduction of the system of racism, there is an ideological or cognitive system dimension which is a representation of social reality based upon group attitudes and identification. In Western capitalist societies, these cognitive systems or ideologies are manipulated by the White elites who seek to maintain their structural dominance over minorities. Thus, the press as an agency of ideological production is controlled by the dominant groups. According to van Dijk this ideological control over minorities includes the *content and structure of the system of ideological ethnic representation*.[3] This is most effectively done by a system of ideological hegemony which seeks acceptance and legitimation of the status quo.

The origins of attitudes, beliefs and behaviour are essentially social in nature. We are not concerned with how ideas are formed and elaborated in the mind of the individual but with how broad currents of ideas are formed as characteristic of a whole phase of social development. It follows from this that those different ideologies are thus developed in the service of different class and ethnic group interests. Van Dijk does not deny the importance of the macro level in shaping historical developments. Nor does he argue that attitudes and beliefs are elements in the micro superstructure with no independence or autonomy being merely reflections of the macroeconomic

2. Van Dijk, *Racism and the Press*.

3. Van Dijk, *Racism and the Press*, 33.

system base. Rather, his argument is that attitudes and beliefs that legitimate behaviour represent a system of ideas characterised by their cognitive consistency. For van Dijk, these ideas are not static, and different periods of industrial development are characterised by different forms of ideological control justifying White dominant group rule and minority obedience.

Following the research of Robert Hood in chapter 4 the most potent way the powerful have of perpetuating their dominance is their control of the images that people in a given society have of themselves. If Black and Asian people are viewed by the majority culture as criminals, what is the use of keeping the laws of that culture? Thus, Black people begin to question their own worth and their position within British society. For the press, the urban disturbances of the 1980s were not popular uprisings but barbarous acts of criminality. These events, comments van Dijk,

> were not seen as caused by ethnic inequality, oppression or discrimination nor as the expression of social economic frustration and rage.[4]

They were nevertheless seen as ethnic events and as such newsworthy. In order to understand how the urban disturbances were seen as an act of barbarous criminality we have only to look at the way the press distorted, misrepresented, and selected the facts of the Handsworth uprising in 1985. They talked of a Black riot and used the word 'tribal'. The *Daily Express* referred to 'Zulu-style' war cries and depicted Black people as golliwogs in cartoon.[5] In order to give focus to the idea of inter-racial conflict between Black and Asian communities, the *Sun* carried the headline "Why West Indians Hate Asians".[6]

According to a researcher writing at the time of these events, the organizing principle of the press is storytelling, and these stories are informed by myths based upon Britain's colonial past.[7] Thus stereotypes are an instant resource in a process of immediate storytelling. However, the stereotypes are limited to Black equals Zulu, older Black, Uncle Tom; Asian equals politically passive and economically shrewd, small businessman. This means that certain stories cannot be told. This is crucial because the structure of

4. Van Dijk, *Racism and the Press*, 2.

5. See Gaffney, "Interpretations of Violence," and *The Daily Express*, 14th October, 1985.

6. See Gaffney, "Interpretations of Violence," and *The Sun*, 12th September, 1985.

7. Gaffney, "Interpretations of Violence."

the story is the agency of explanation. The stories that are untold remain so not simply because they might push interpretations towards a class analysis or give credibility to political actors, but because they undermine the explanatory characteristics of certain of the essential resource in storytelling.

We can account for the role of the press in the reproduction of racism in British society by relating its structure to other institutions within British society. The elite groups control the press not only in the sense of their ownership of the ideological means of production, but also in terms of their access to its structures. The way that news is gathered together with what is considered to be newsworthy are both determined by organisational routines and powerful interest groups, which are professional and ideological in nature. Powerful elite groups can bring pressure to bear in both political and financial senses. Furthermore, members of elite groups are themselves prominent news actors and for this reason their actions are newsworthy. So, their opinions are sought and presented as credible and legitimate. So confident are the ruling elites of their ideological position of superiority over minority groups that they can afford to allow a certain measure of opposition and dissent. Thus, elite groups, in Western capitalist societies, gain access to the media through the reproduction of power relationships.

The media can reproduce racism by setting the agenda and affecting public reaction to particular events. Clearly the press is manipulated by those who have access to its structures. These elite groups include politicians and professional media personnel. However, the question always arises regarding whether the media creates the social reality or merely reflects it. It could be claimed that even if it doesn't create the social reality, it definitely reinforces attitudes already either formed or in the process of formation. The role of the media in the reproduction of racism cannot be seen in isolation from the racialisation process which describes the presence of Black and Asian people in British society in terms of immigrant host relationships. These relationships were discussed in chapter 2 as part of the single British identify idea and again in more detail in chapter 4 in the context of the racialised other concept of Black Theology. Immigrant host relationships are ideological and can be translated at the micro level into routines of newsgathering. In this the press does not necessarily reflect racism or initiate it but rather, as an institution in British society, the press must be seen as a participant in the racialisation process.

The mid-1990s, a decade after the Brixton uprisings, saw two nights of civil disturbances in the city of Bradford, UK. I was a vicar in Bradford at the time, so what follows is my personal knowledge and reflection upon these events. Imran Merbhan was on his way to the mosque for evening prayer when he saw a police car accelerate, brake and come to a grinding halt, trapping a young lad's foot under its wheels. Two police officers got out and began laughing, according to several eyewitnesses. Imran went up and remonstrated with the police. Meanwhile Javed Iqbal came out of his house to see what was happening. One of the officers chased him back into his house, confronting Iqbal and his sister, who was carrying her eight-month-old daughter. A scuffle broke out. One of the police officers is alleged to have struck the young mother. The police arrested Imran and the pace of events gathered momentum with a grim inevitability. Other arrests followed including that of Taj Hussein, a well-respected local teacher. He was arrested when he went to the police station on Toller Lane to try to negotiate a cooling down of tensions. He was cuffed so tightly that his hands went blue. At the national level, no questions were asked that I ever saw in the national media about who really caused the outbreak of community distress that led to the disruption; nor was the conduct of the police seriously questioned. On the Monday after the weekend disturbances, at Bradford University where I was a visiting lecturer, I found myself to be the only member of the Social Sciences department to be available to the local news media. I was interviewed on two radio stations where I explained that the disturbance was the result of, at the very least, institutionalised racism.

The local MP at the time, Max Madden, seemed to be blaming the disturbances on a plague of prostitution accompanied by the inevitable crime and drugs problem. The whole area of Manningham in Bradford was blighted with the attendant malasie which hurt and upset the devout in the area. Islamic people had challenged these activities in their area because they offend natural morality. As in Balsall Heath in Birmingham, local people took to the streets in order to move the prostitutes, their pimps and clients on. Local feeling then in Manningham on this issue was exacerbated by the television series *Band of Gold*, with a storyline featuring prostitution, which drew greater numbers than usual into the lanes. The Church of England rector for Manningham further offended decent citizens by calling for prostitution to be decriminalised. Local Muslims who I spoke to could not believe that any religious leader could possibly condone such activities. What could I say to them? That the majority White society forces its outsiders and its rejects into the ghettoes just as the Victorians covered the legs of tables and pianos?

Conclusion

Following the Stephen Lawrence Enquiry,[8] questions were asked about the treatment of Black people in the institutions of British society including the police, social services, education and the churches. However, can these questions continue to be asked today without Black people being seen as the cause of the problem? Stephen Lawrence was the victim of a racially motivated murder in which the police failed to conduct an adequate investigation, failed even to offer immediate relief to a young man lying helpless on the street. Here the concept of institutionalised racism comes into its own since some institutions like trade unions are able to amplify racist belief systems through long-established practices which have the effect of excluding Black and Asian trade unionists. It is precisely when 'race' is not mentioned and there is no overt intention to discriminate that the action of policy makers can have a detrimental effect on Muslim and Hindu workplace groupings.

• • •

According to Anthony Reddie, not to be White in British society is to be othered and marginalised to the realms of obscurity whereby everything that identifies you as a person is rubbished by that society.[9] Englishness and Britishness are often defined by what they exclude, finding support in this approach by a desperate appeal to what is understood to be a Judeo-Christian heritage even though that identity is not owned by the nation or church. Reddie makes the point that the Jewish identity of the Jesus of history requires an engagement with otherness in a way that the Christ of faith approach does not.[10] The downside to this identity crisis, within White Euro American Christianity, for us as the racialised other, is the ability of White Christianity not only to hide our existence as a positive presence in church and society but to demonise Blackness as something that does not belong to either. In practical terms, this pathology of the other involves stereotyping us as the enemy within.

As I have already indicated, Black theology challenges the idea of constructing difference as a series of binary opposition in which White is the defining term and Black the dependent category. Within Western thought and language, Whiteness is then a neural yardstick or cultural marker against which everything else is defined. Its hegemony as a privileged signifier

8. "Stephen Lawrence Inquiry."
9. Reddie, *Working Against the Grain*, 139.
10. Reddie, *Working Against the Grain*, 147.

marginalises everything else in the social matrix as the colonial other. Witness then, in this context is the universal cultural norm, which seeks control, to manipulate and commodify Blackness. It is a parasitic and political category for that purpose. We have already concluded that Whiteness has no consciousness of its own and only exists asymmetrically in opposition to subordinate other categories. Furthermore, people do not rush to identify with Whiteness largely because they don't have to. The only exception would be those who have a particular interest, such as holding and articulating overtly racist views. Thus, Whiteness does not have to explain itself, justify itself or seek definition because it has no boundaries of its own except in opposition to what is not White. Historically Whiteness permeates European culture as a defining agent of creating colonial others, projecting on to them inferiority and self-hatred. For this reason, White identities are difficult to take seriously and have been characterised by contradiction, fragmentation and disintegration as seen through imaginary dramas and narratives. Thus, White groups prefer to identify and define themselves as English, Welsh, Scottish and Irish. The White male hegemony is threatened by, and is linked in opposition to anything perceived to be Black and feminist.

Whiteness can be challenged through the Deconstruction of what I mean by Englishness. In chapter 2 there was considerable interest around what constituted Englishness in the context of the Big Society initiative of modern Conservatism following the new Labour area. So should we give some consideration as to whether a distinction should be made between Saxon and Celtic heritage in terms of the White population of the UK. I raise this question in the context of how we use the generic term British to incorporate English, Welsh, Scots and Irish groups.

There has been a heavy investment in Welsh nationalism and language. Welsh language is often promoted by people who sound very middle-class and English. Sometimes they are university professors and clergy who take up senior jobs in England and upon retirement return to their native land and then find fault with everything that is pertained to be English. From a Black perspective, when our willingness to learn a foreign language is used as an entry requirement for clergy and lay posts it becomes a discriminatory practice. It is White people who like language studies and have the privileged access to these skills. Clearly this must be challenged and identified as a discriminatory practice as such institutionalised racism.

At no time were the islands that make up the United Kingdom described exclusively as England despite the perceived dominance of English culture radiating out of London and the home counties. Unsurprisingly, the outcomes are expressed in platitudes and stereotypes with the Celts deemed emotional and irrational whilst the calm English remain majestically reasonable. Added English virtues include moderation, tolerance, general all-round decency and understated modesty. Perhaps this last explains the English love of the cult of the amateur, even to the indulging of the harmlessly eccentric. All this accompanied by a dry sense of humor. Viewed from the Celtic standpoint, the English are not seen in the way they self-describe but as coldly patronizing, proud. The Celtic fringe, it is claimed, is forced, it would seem, to define itself in opposition to the normative English. But if England is the norm, why would the English have to describe themselves to themselves, or to anyone for that matter, and certainly not the other nationality groups that make up the United Kingdom? From a Black perspective the United Kingdom is a very loose grouping of White communities who no longer have an empire to maintain, so we should not be surprised they have time on their hands to be in opposition to each other.

In sum, Whiteness has been successful in associating Black people with criminality and social degeneracy. This was seen clearly in the publicity surrounding the so-called Rodney King trial in America even though he was victim and not instigator of police violence. Whiteness is responsible for the continuance of racial stereotypes and myths that surround the concept of 'race' where Black people are identified as a category. Their alleged traits, as well as being characteristic of their group, are also seen as the cause of many troubles destabilizing the majority cultural norm. Whiteness is not an historical concept any more than Blackness is a homogenizing category. However, its effectiveness in defining and controlling the colonial other can been seen in historically and materially specific contexts as already discussed in chapter 4. Thus, the alienating experience of colonialism continues to define Black and Asian identities and restrict the right to self-determination.

• • •

So, Britishness, including the Anglican aspect of that identity, became an oppositional culture to European Roman Catholicism. The British, thus used to polarised relationships, automatically viewed the arrival of Afro Caribbeans with defensiveness, at the least, and, at the most, hostility. The devious practices of exclusion were an entirely predictable response to the generous helpers of the Windrush era who came at the homeland's call but not to the British desire. But the British were polite, Blacks were not thrown out of the parish churches they presented themselves at, they were told to stand at the back!

So, the Church of England, as a religious and cultural signifier of Englishness and Britishness, drew its skirts around itself, harking for those nostalgic and mythical certainties, disturbed by the intrusive presence of reality, as Patrick Wright explores in his notion of *Deep England*. Today, while the central position of the Church of England in the life of the nation is under question, yet the Anglican presence is expected at major national moments. Coronations cannot occur without the blessing of the Church of England; the archbishop is expected to be able to comment at the drop of a hat upon a range of diverse events and situations. Is it any surprise, with the complex, brutal and violent history of the English career across the global stage, that the institution that the English use to represent itself to itself is in a state of conflict and fracture. In that, it truly and ironically does represent the life of the nation.

The United Kingdom remains a highly discriminatory place to live despite significant changes in the mode of expression of xenophobia and racist intolerance. Thus, this reality and its consequences for Black and Asian communities, remains the context within which faith organisation operate. This book has explored the mode of involvement of the racialised other in the Faith Workers' Branch of Unite the Union which has been shaped not just by their experience of individualised racial prejudice but, more importantly, by instutionalised practices that work again them. It is the values and norms which form part of Englishness and not trade union values, that governs the treatment of non-White members and hence their mode of involvement within this institution. I can only conclude that the Faith Worker Branch is not fit for purpose as a faith organisation since it only gives recognition and support to members who belong to historic White churches. Today the Faith Workers' Branch of Unite is governed by an Executive Committee of five people from these churches. There is no representation on this Executive Committee for Muslim and Hindu work place groupings who must now seek permission from the chair before initiating any actions of their own.

So, what about the ministry of the racialised other? What words of encouragement could I offer to Black and Asian trade unionists who might consider church ministry. The same advice I would give to Muslim and Hindu trade unionists who consider working for a faith organisation. Justice is a future aspiration born out of the agonies of the present and dissonance of the past. Therefore, whatever you do for justice and equality, it is worth doing. In my own faith and denomination, the Church of England, ordained ministry is important because it is the meeting point of many ministries. However even if Black and Asian clergy get appointed to incumbencies it does not follow that the Church will want to foster their professional development in the same way as those of our White colleagues. In my PhD research I interviewed a number of older Black and Asian clergy who questioned who is looking out for them as they sat there while less experienced White clergy were promoted over them. For a number of years now I have seen many of the White colleagues I went to college with being promoted to the middle management and senior positions in the Church—residential canon, diocesan director of ordinands, archdeacon, cathedral dean and bishop. I am not saying there are no Black and Asian clergy in these jobs. What I am saying is that there are few of us in positions of responsibility and this is disproportionate with the growing numbers of Black and Asian congregations. Furthermore, when non-White clergy do get promotion, they are not always the best qualified and as such are unlikely to promote other so-called ethnic minorities more able than themselves. This is how the system works to marginalise the racialised other.

It is a good thing that most Black and Asian clergy do not go into ministry to get on and advance their careers, otherwise they would be disappointed. At my theological college it was easy to spot the ones who were destined for high office because they were those who did not attend local churches on Sunday morning. They were also more likely to have been to public schools and come into training with their own financial means. There are serious issues of justice here and the church should give responsibility to its personnel based on a genuine calling, evidenced by the ability to do the job required. Too many of our procedures are clothed in obscurity. We need a transparent appointment system, which should contain marginalised people at least on its long lists for all middle management and senior appointments. I published an article on this subject, "Black Clergy Discontent" in the *Contemporary Journal of Religion* over three decades ago. I have had no feedback from those who make these decisions.

So, what about the Faith Workers' Branch? Is it fit for purpose? The answer is 'no' but having identified the problem, what can we do about it? How do we get White majority trade unions to stop treating us as the other, that which does not fit their norm and assigns us the category of deviant? I can start with the Christian Bible and commend to them Luke 10:25–37 and the Good Samaritan. Christians have few commandments given to them by Jesus, love God and love your neighbour as yourself.

The Good Samaritan is a well-known and much-loved parable.[11] It is framed by the questioner who is very ready to challenge Jesus as to what he can do to attain eternal life even though he already knows the answer. You might like to think about what is going on there and whether we ever do the same. Are we calling out to God about the way forward when we already know the answer? In this, dear reader, what are we avoiding? Jesus drew upon well-understood figures in his contemporary society, people who had clear expectations upon them, and he reverses those, the clever storyteller that he is. I wonder what figures he would use today? I can see Anglican bishops, trade union officers, and bankers. I can also see the Samaritan slot be taken by someone like the Australian Sikh who a few years ago unhesitatingly unwound his turban as a lifeline to extend to someone drowning? Sikhs must keep their kesh, or 'hair', covered when outside the home but some things are more urgent than ritual rules. This gesture went viral, to the astonishment of the young man.

One aspect of this parable is particularly important: The Samaritan was prepared. He carried his equivalent of a first-aid kit, and he was ready not to look away. He took action. So, when Jesus ends his story by saying to his questioner 'Go and do the same', he is laying down a very clear imperative to us all. Now if we take this parable on its own, it might end there, but what Jesus does next is telling. He makes a pastoral visit to Mary and Martha. Mary is prayerful and pays attention to their visitor whereas Martha bustles around, active but not taking effective kingdom-enriching action. So, questions are raised about the relationship between prayer and deeds. Based on the two Great Commandments, we can see a virtuous circle of loving God, being in a nurturing relationship with God, feeding on God's beauty and glory, but then taking that energy, like the Samaritan, and joining God in the divine rescue mission.

Prayer is our dialogue with God: purposeful action is God's dialogue with the world through us. In these troubled times—and when aren't they troubled?—we need to show whether we are Marthas, busy moving specks of dust around, or rescuers, reaching out into this suffering world and changing things. Doing those good works prepared for us to walk in because if we don't, those works will not get done and countless opportunities will be lost. And always remember, we do not act alone. We have each other.

11. Luke 10:25–37.

But more importantly we have the everlasting arms of God girding us up to be God's voice, hands and heart. And all of this here and now to betoken the world to come when all should be bound up and made whole.

• • •

We have to engage with the biblical text and the theology that comes from them in order to make sense of these concepts, particularly our neighbour. Black theology is about how we sharpen this understanding. Who is my neighbour? Who am I? What is a person? These questions are all closely linked. In God, all our barriers are broken down and a type of unity both terrifying and beautiful is ushered in. In God, cause and effect are brought together in a way that invites us to take some true control. For if the White majority trade union movement truly takes on board the idea of neighbour, then no one is a distant entity anymore. Everyone becomes an intimate part of our own selves because we are caught up equally in the redeeming and suffering love of God. A true Christian believer who happens to be also a member of the Faith Workers' Branch cannot become a cruel person and exploit others in obvious or subtle ways because what they do to the least of these my kinsfolk, they know they do to God who is our ultimate kinsperson. They cannot alienate another person and regard them as less human than themselves because they should know that they are, as we are all made in the image of God and redeemed in the blood of Christ. And this is where Christian trade unionists at last begin to find an answer to our question: who is my neighbour? For if we are each of us doubly a reflection of the divine reality, being made by God and rescued through Christ, then my neighbour is precious beyond belief. Until Anglicans and Methodists within the Faith Workers' Branch treat their neighbour with all the respect that they deep down know that they should, then they are denying the image of God within us and within themselves.

Black theology seeks to discover the divinity within each person. Then it takes stock of how we regard people and what expectations we have for their treatment and for their status within society. We must look into the eyes of those who share the world with us and remember what else they share. They share a birthright in the effective and transforming love of God.

And Finally . . .

So, what is the significance of doing theology from a particular cultural perspective? Whenever someone speaks or writes to describe any important event, they write from the point of view of their own language, culture and time. We know from the biblical work we did earlier that this might mean that their version of events might seem very different if it were to happen today to us. But what of our own time? How do we proclaim our faith in God? In our Western culture, we tend to think of ourselves as being composed of mind and body, visible and invisible. We feel that what endures after death is the mind or spirit part of ourselves and that our bodies perish. Therefore, we are split and our two halves do not always get on well together. We also see ourselves as distinct and separate entities who can lose touch with ourselves if we deny ourselves the right to self-expression. If I said that I was going on retreat to find myself then you would know exactly what I mean. This seeking to understand my individual identity approach is not globally the case. Other cultures and traditions have different anthropologies that have much to teach us about communion and group identity.

So, what of my own context? I come from a high church liberal Christian background. I was born in Windsor, Berkshire, UK. The gifts that I bring to ministry are particular to my ethnicity and culture as a Black, Anglican priest. These gifts enable me to question the so-called normal. I am not so much an outsider looking in, rather I am an insider looking out and I do not always like what I see. I have a culture of challenge and civil disobedience. Being a person of faith should make you an alien in any culture.

• • •

God empowers and consoles us. Our prayers to God urge and implore. As people of faith, we call the same call and sing the same song: that of redemption, of restoration, of life made whole again, justice and peace. For this reason, we cannot live complacent lives but we must be stirred up, restless for God, restless for the best for our fellow creatures and for our universe. As faith workers we believe God is the creator of all things, and that God had a purpose in creating the world. There is a supreme purpose in life, this life is incomplete in itself, and it will find its completion in the fullness of eternal life with God. But quite a lot can happen before then.

Bibliography

Allport, Gordon, and Bernard Krammer. "Some Roots of Prejudice." *Journal of Psychology* 22 (1946) 9–39.

Allport, Gordon, and Michael Ross. "Personal Religious Orientation and Prejudice." *Journal of Personality and Social Psychology* 5 (1967) 432–43.

Bagley, Christopher. "Relation of Religion and Racial Prejudice in Europe." *Scientific Study of Religion* 9.3 (1970) 219–25.

Bishop, Matthew, and Michael Green. *The Road from Ruin: A New Capitalism for a Big Society.* New York: Black, 2010.

Blond, Philip. *Red Tory: How Left and Right Have Broken Britain and How We Can Fix It.* London: Faber & Faber, 2010.

Byron, Gay. *Symbolic Blackness and Ethnic Difference in Early Christian Literature.* London: Routledge, 2002.

Carpenter, Humphrey. *Robert Runcie.* London: Hodder & Stoughton, 1996.

Colley, Linda. *Britons.* Great Britain: Vintage, 1992

Curtis, Lewis. *Anglo-Saxons and Celts: A Study of Anti-Irish Prejudice in Victorian England.* New York: New York University Press, 1968.

Frazier, Franklin. *Black Bourgeoisie.* New York: Free Press, 1957.

Fryer, Peter. *Staying Power: The History of Black People in Britain.* London: Pluto, 1984.

Gaffney, John. "Interpretations of Violence: The Handsworth Riots of 1985." Policy Papers in Ethnic Relations, ESRC, 1987.

Gilroy, Paul. *There Ain't No Black in the Union Jack.* London: Hutchinson, 1987.

Gorsuch, Richard, and Daniel Aleshire. "Christian Faith and Prejudice: A Review and Interpretation of Research." *Journal for the Scientific Study of Religion* 13 (1974) 281–307.

Gratus, Jack. *The Great White Lie: Slavery, Emancipation and Changing Racial Attitudes,* London: Hutchinson, 1973.

Hardin, John, et al. *Prejudice and Ethnic Relations.* Handbook of Social Psychology. Reading, MA: Addison-Wesley, 1954.

Harris, Raymund. *Scriptural Researches on the Licitness of the Slave-Trade: Shewing Its Conformity with the Principles of Natural and Revealed Religion, Delineated in the Sacred Writings of the Word of God*. 1788. Fascimile edition, Liverpool, UK: N.p., 2015.

Hetchter, Michael. *Internal Colonialism: The Celtic Fringe in British National Development, 1536–1966*. London: Routledge & Paul, 1975.

Hood, Robert. *Begrimed and Black: Christian Traditions on Black People and Blackness*. Minneapolis: Fortress, 1994.

Jordan, Winthrop. *White over Black*. New York: Norton, 1968.

King, Morton, and Richard Hunt. *Measuring Religious Dimensions: Studies of Congregational Involvement*. Dallas, TX: Congregational Involvement Study, 1972.

Lenski, Gerhard. *The Religious Factor*. 2nd ed. Garden City, NY: Doublesday, 1963.

Morrish, Ivor. *The Background of Immigrant Children*. London: Allen & Unwin, 1971.

Norman, Jesse. *The Big Society: The Anatomy of the New Politics*. Buckingham: The University of Buckingham Press, 2010.

Palmer, Bernard. *High & Mitred: A Study of Prime Ministers as Bishop-Makers 1837–1977*. London: SPCK, 1992.

Park, Robert. *Race and Culture*. New York: The Free Press, 1950.

———. "Sociology." In *Research in the Social Sciences: Its Fundamental Methods and Objectives*, edited by Wilson Gee, 3–49. New York: Macmillan, 1929.

Parry, Henry. "Protestants, Catholics and Prejudice." *International Journal for Opinion and Attitude Research* 3 (1949) 205–13.

Patterson, Sheila. *Dark Strangers: A Study of West Indians in London*. Harmondsworth: Penguin, 1965.

Photiadis, John, and Arthur Johnson. "Orthodoxy, Church Participation, and Authoritarianism." *American Journal of Sociology* 69 (1963) 244–48.

Ragan, Roger. "Attitudes of White Methodist Church Members in Selected Los Angeles Metropolitan Area Churches towards Residential Segregation of the Negro." *Dissertation Abstracts* 24 (1963) n.p.

Reddie, Anthony. *Working Against the Grain: Re-imaging Black Theology in the 12st Century*. London: Equinox, 2008.

Rokeach, Milton. "Value Systems in Religion." *Review of Religious Research* 11 (1969) 24–39.

Sharp, Granville. *Essays*. London: N.p., 1776.

Shiner, Gregory, and Charles Ford. "The Relation of Ethnocentric Attitudes to Intensity of Religious Practice." *Journal of Educational Sociology* 32 (1958) 157–62.

"The Stephen Lawrence Inquiry: Report of an Inquiry by Sir William Macpherson of Cluny." https://assets.publishing.service.gov.uk/government/uploads/system/uploads/attachment_data/file/277111/4262.pdf.

"Swann Report (1985)." http://www.educationengland.org.uk/documents/swann/swann1985.html.

Van Dijk, Teun. *Racism and the Press*. London: Routledge, 1991.

Wilkinson, Richard. *The Impact of Inequality: How to Make Sick Societies Healthier*. London: Routledge, 2005.

Wilkinson, Richard, and Kate Pickett. *The Spirit Level*. London: Penguin, 2010.

Williams, Eric. *Capitalism & Slavery*. New York: Russell & Russell, 1944.

Wilson, A. N. "Doing the Lambeth Walk." *The Spectator*, November 12th, 1983.

Wright, Patrick. *On Living in an Old Country*. Rev. ed. Oxford: Oxford University Press, 2009.